Student Workbook

AGS PUBLISHING

Basic Math Skills

by
August V. Treff
and
Donald H. Jacobs

Wieser Educational

30281 Esperanza
Rancho Santa Margarita, CA 92688-2130
1 (800) 880-4433 ♦ Fax (800) 949-0209

www.wieser-ed.com ♦ Email info@wieser-ed.com

Printed in the United States of America

ISBN 0-7854-2954-9
Product Number 93563

A 0 9 8 7 6 5

Table of Contents

Place Value

EXAMPLE Look at the place of the underlined digit.
Write the name of the place of the underlined digit.   1<u>9</u>8 ___tens___

Directions Write the name of the place for each underlined digit.

1. 2,4<u>0</u>6 _____
2. 12<u>8</u> _____
3. 70,<u>8</u>35 _____
4. 17,<u>5</u>01 _____
5. 301,33<u>9</u> _____
6. 10,0<u>0</u>2 _____
7. 49<u>1</u>,918 _____
8. 46,<u>0</u>23 _____
9. <u>6</u>,005 _____
10. 59,<u>7</u>00 _____
11. <u>3</u>4,000 _____
12. 500,<u>0</u>69 _____
13. <u>3</u>41 _____
14. 1<u>0</u>,000 _____
15. 1,0<u>0</u>0,000 _____
16. 3,<u>9</u>02,885 _____
17. <u>5</u>03 _____
18. 16,<u>0</u>30 _____
19. <u>2</u>,000,003 _____
20. 73,9<u>9</u>9 _____

21. 29<u>4</u> _____
22. 5,<u>0</u>20,007 _____
23. 9<u>1</u>9,078 _____
24. 4,<u>0</u>09 _____
25. 5,6<u>8</u>3 _____
26. 687,6<u>3</u>3 _____
27. 48,04<u>0</u> _____
28. 384,9<u>9</u>5 _____
29. 8,<u>8</u>37 _____
30. 23,0<u>0</u>0,821 _____
31. <u>1</u>,010,001 _____
32. 5<u>3</u> _____
33. 5,0<u>7</u>8 _____
34. <u>7</u>08,583 _____
35. 61,2<u>2</u>2 _____
36. <u>7</u>01,865 _____
37. 70,7<u>3</u>8 _____
38. 5<u>0</u>1,775 _____
39. 102,8<u>9</u>5 _____
40. 71,99<u>0</u> _____

41. 88,2<u>1</u>0 _____
42. 9<u>0</u>,909 _____
43. <u>2</u>03,872,221 _____
44. <u>9</u>10,573 _____
45. 10,7<u>1</u>0 _____
46. 7<u>3</u>7,098 _____
47. <u>4</u>0,910 _____
48. 10,0<u>0</u>2 _____
49. <u>9</u>,033,921 _____
50. 8<u>1</u>0,022,033 _____
51. 3<u>0</u>0,941 _____
52. 2,<u>6</u>71 _____
53. 94,<u>7</u>24 _____
54. <u>8</u>03,921 _____
55. <u>5</u>06 _____
56. 1,<u>0</u>34 _____
57. 9<u>2</u>0 _____
58. 1,0<u>2</u>3 _____
59. 46<u>2</u>,987 _____
60. 10,<u>9</u>35 _____

Writing Numbers

EXAMPLE   Read the numeral. Write the numeral in words.

1,241 _____one thousand, two hundred forty-one_____

Directions Write the following numerals in words.

1. 1,208 _____

_____

2. 204 _____

_____

3. 4,801 _____

_____

4. 80,026 _____

_____

5. 92,224 _____

_____

6. 44,659 _____

_____

7. 602,875 _____

_____

8. 6,096,089 _____

_____

9. 673,218,003 _____

_____

10. 830,002 _____

_____

Number Translations

Read the amount written in words. Write the numeral for the amount.

Four thousand, one hundred ninety-two   ___4,192___

Directions Write the following amounts in numerals.

1. Three thousand, five hundred thirty-six   _____

2. Five hundred six   _____

3. Seven hundred forty-nine   _____

4. Five thousand, nine   _____

5. Seven thousand, three hundred twenty-one   _____

6. Nine thousand, two   _____

7. Nine thousand, five hundred   _____

8. Thirty-one thousand, four   _____

9. Fifty-seven thousand, nine hundred   _____

10. Eighty thousand, six hundred thirty-two   _____

11. Forty-two thousand, three   _____

12. Ninety-one thousand, four hundred eleven   _____

13. Seven hundred thousand   _____

14. Nine hundred thousand, sixty-four   _____

15. Seven hundred seventy-one thousand, five hundred forty-nine   _____

16. Four hundred fifty-five million   _____

17. Three hundred five million, twenty-eight thousand, two   _____

18. Eight thousand, eleven   _____

19. Three hundred sixty-three thousand, five hundred four   _____

20. Seventy thousand, nine hundred forty-two   _____

Rounding Whole Numbers

EXAMPLE   Read the number. Round the number to the nearest tens place.
Round numbers 5–9 up. Round numbers 1–4 down.

26 = ___30___

Directions Round these numbers to the nearest tens place.

1. 48 = _____

2. 305 = _____

3. 4,056 = _____

4. 408 = _____

5. 9,911 = _____

6. 72,099 = _____

7. 5 = _____

8. 803 = _____

9. 617 = _____

10. 61,092 = _____

11. 777 = _____

12. 290 = _____

13. 4 = _____

14. 18 = _____

15. 102,005 = _____

16. 4,506 = _____

17. 9 = _____

18. 61 = _____

Directions Round these numbers to the nearest hundreds place.

19. 693 = _____

20. 349 = _____

21. 9,012 = _____

22. 7,521 = _____

23. 43,071 = _____

24. 102,009 = _____

25. 29 = _____

26. 3,002,091 = _____

27. 71 = _____

28. 91,029 = _____

29. 6,018 = _____

30. 33,951 = _____

31. 34,988 = _____

32. 89 = _____

33. 129,999 = _____

34. 10,891 = _____

35. 509 = _____

36. 780 = _____

Directions Round these numbers to the nearest thousands place.

37. 199 = _____

38. 499 = _____

39. 1,500 = _____

40. 25,509 = _____

41. 999 = _____

42. 90,098 = _____

43. 1,058 = _____

44. 501 = _____

45. 99 = _____

46. 301 = _____

47. 298 = _____

48. 78,475 = _____

49. 470,512 = _____

50. 19,000 = _____

Addition of Whole Numbers

EXAMPLE   Write the problem in vertical form. Add.

18 + 162 + 171 + 8 = _____359_____

$$
\begin{array}{r}
{}^{1\,1}\\
18\\
162\\
171\\
+\ \ 8\\
\hline
359
\end{array}
$$

Directions Rewrite the following addends in the vertical form and add.

1. 32 + 141 + 68 + 122 = _____

2. 4 + 37 + 812 + 774 + 1 = _____

3. 8 + 35 + 77 + 273 + 65 = _____

4. 54 + 76 + 90 + 725 = _____

5. 701 + 33 + 83 + 61 + 374 = _____

6. 7 + 837 + 504 + 91 + 522 = _____

7. 93 + 705 + 866 + 73 = _____

8. 45 + 38 + 401 + 5,000 = _____

9. 86 + 59 + 63 + 27 + 105 = _____

10. 395 + 57 + 82 + 273 + 88 = _____

11. 304 + 771 + 826 + 776 = _____

12. 366 + 8,261 + 8,837 + 912 = _____

13. 6,372 + 75 + 908 + 76 = _____

14. 874 + 7,601 + 406 + 837 = _____

15. 7,091 + 5,308 + 354 + 34

16. 645 + 823 + 806 + 7,73

17. 6,657 + 4,321 + 7,341

18. 905 + 624 + 861 + 968 = _____

19. 6,241 + 8,548 + 9,092 = _____

20. 558 + 523 + 128 + 8,241 = _____

21. 264 + 63 + 7,253 + 2 = _____

22. 73 + 8,263 + 78 + 521 = _____

23. 42 + 3,547 + 8,142 + 467 = _____

24. 8,263 + 990 + 352 + 37 = _____

25. 7,364 + 364 + 902 + 36 = _____

26. 889 + 902 + 836 + 2,431 = _____

390 + 263 + 7,746 + 477 = _____

+ 9,928 + 388 = _____

6 = _____

+ 3,745 = _____

116 = _____

11 + 2,883 = _____

39 = _____

(handwritten note on sticky paper: "Give this work to D'andre Brown")

Directions Solve the following word problems with addition.

34. Mark collects 178 pounds of scrap iron and 8_ pounds of copper. Find the total weight of the metal.

_____

35. Tara purchases 280 square feet of carpet for her living room and 250 square feet for her bedroom. Find the total number of square feet she purchases.

_____

Subtraction of Whole Numbers

EXAMPLE Write the problem in vertical form. Subtract.

From 821 subtract 71. ___750___

$$\begin{array}{r}712\\ \cancel{8}\cancel{2}1\\ -\ 71\\ \hline 750\end{array}$$

Directions Rewrite these subtraction problems in the vertical form. Then subtract.

1. 694 − 22 = _____
2. From 384 subtract 75. _____
3. 602 − 113 = _____
4. From 102 subtract 89. _____
5. 856 − 773 = _____
6. Subtract 871 from 1,029. _____
7. 552 − 498 = _____
8. Subtract 528 from 717. _____
9. 4,852 − 665 = _____
10. From 3,810 subtract 1,922. _____
11. 3,952 − 3,877 = _____
12. Subtract 9,099 from 10,099. _____
13. 12,923 − 8,973 = _____
14. From 16,242 subtract 10,987. _____

15. 3,049 − 1,906 = _____
16. Subtract 786 from 25,004. _____
17. 46,974 − 18,860 = _____
18. From 65,208 subtract 56,987. _____
19. 7,890 − 5,699 = _____
20. Subtract 61,098 from 87,987. _____
21. 67,951 − 56,508 = _____
22. From 10,001 subtract 9,802. _____
23. 78,000 − 6,784 = _____
24. Subtract 675 from 1,000. _____
25. 362,900 − 87,098 = _____
26. Subtract 81,321 from 601,030. _____
27. 70,981 − 69,673 = _____
28. From 508,821 subtract 91,055. _____

Directions Solve the following word problems with subtraction.

29. Van sells 185 tickets to the school's Staff Talent Show. If he was given 350 tickets to sell, how many does he have left to sell? _____

30. Cassie plans a 475-mile trip. She drives 296 miles the first day. How many miles must she drive the second day to complete her trip? _____

Multiplication Practice

EXAMPLE Multiply the number in the left column by the number in the top row.

$$\begin{array}{c|c} & 4 \\ \hline 3 & 12 \end{array}$$

Directions Fill in the multiplication facts. Multiply each number in the left column by each number on the top row. Write the product of each pair of numbers in the box where the column and the row meet.

1.

×	0	1	2	3	4	5	6	7	8	9	10
0	0	0	0								
1	0	1	2								
2											
3											
4											
5											
6											
7											
8											
9											
10											

2.

×	6	2	3	0	9	10	8	7	5	4	1
2											
9											
5											
4											
8											
0											
7											
6											
3											
1											
10											

Multiplication by Powers of Ten

EXAMPLES
When you multiply a number by 10, write the number.
Then write a zero at the end. $235 \times 10 = 2,350$

When you multiply a number by 100, write the number.
Then write two zeros at the end. $235 \times 100 = 23,500$

When you multiply a number by 1,000, write the number.
Then write three zeros at the end. $235 \times 1,000 = 235,000$

Directions Multiply by these powers of ten.

1. $325 \times 10 =$ _____	**21.** $412 \times 1,000 =$ _____
2. $421 \times 100 =$ _____	**22.** $906 \times 1,000 =$ _____
3. $4,631 \times 10 =$ _____	**23.** $10,802 \times 100 =$ _____
4. $6,023 \times 100 =$ _____	**24.** $104 \times 100 =$ _____
5. $702 \times 100 =$ _____	**25.** $56 \times 10 =$ _____
6. $3,011 \times 1,000 =$ _____	**26.** $13 \times 100 =$ _____
7. $3,203 \times 100 =$ _____	**27.** $9 \times 1,000 =$ _____
8. $26,190 \times 10 =$ _____	**28.** $83 \times 1,000 =$ _____
9. $1,043 \times 100 =$ _____	**29.** $183 \times 1,000 =$ _____
10. $50,783 \times 1,000 =$ _____	**30.** $7 \times 1,000 =$ _____
11. $72 \times 1,000 =$ _____	**31.** $801 \times 100 =$ _____
12. $38 \times 1,000 =$ _____	**32.** $334 \times 10 =$ _____
13. $106 \times 100 =$ _____	**33.** $632 \times 10 =$ _____
14. $81 \times 100 =$ _____	**34.** $4,567 \times 100 =$ _____
15. $4,123 \times 10 =$ _____	**35.** $5 \times 100 =$ _____
16. $3,007 \times 1,000 =$ _____	**36.** $20,304 \times 100 =$ _____
17. $962 \times 1,000 =$ _____	**37.** $100 \times 1,000 =$ _____
18. $300 \times 10 =$ _____	**38.** $20,011 \times 100 =$ _____
19. $4,305 \times 10 =$ _____	**39.** $4,302 \times 100 =$ _____
20. $4,020 \times 1,000 =$ _____	**40.** $10,001 \times 100 =$ _____

Multiplication of Whole Numbers

EXAMPLE Write the problem in vertical form. Multiply.

$52 \times 42 = $ _____2,184_____

$$
\begin{array}{r}
52 \\
\times\ 42 \\
\hline
104 \\
+\ 208 \\
\hline
2{,}184
\end{array}
$$

Directions Rewrite these multiplication problems in the vertical form and multiply.

1. $24 \times 22 = $ _____

2. $61 \times 18 = $ _____

3. $201 \times 43 = $ _____

4. $85 \times 72 = $ _____

5. $712 \times 66 = $ _____

6. $819 \times 94 = $ _____

7. $465 \times 20 = $ _____

8. $762 \times 300 = $ _____

9. $301 \times 300 = $ _____

10. $784 \times 100 = $ _____

11. $629 \times 150 = $ _____

12. $607 \times 515 = $ _____

13. $5,763 \times 501 = $ _____

14. $7,114 \times 35 = $ _____

15. $920 \times 724 = $ _____

16. $856 \times 326 = $ _____

17. $3,021 \times 307 = $ _____

18. $638 \times 800 = $ _____

19. $4,160 \times 110 = $ _____

20. $8,522 \times 574 = $ _____

21. $5,021 \times 4,000 = $ _____

22. $7,000 \times 387 = $ _____

23. $5,448 \times 673 = $ _____

24. $7,361 \times 6,000 = $ _____

25. $4,000 \times 3,000 = $ _____

26. $4,000 \times 4,000 = $ _____

27. $3,500 \times 5,100 = $ _____

28. $6,702 \times 1,023 = $ _____

Directions Solve the following word problems with multiplication.

29. Leah runs 4 miles every day before school for exercise. If she runs 179 days, how many miles will she run?

_____

30. Each student in Mr. Brown's class donates 15 sandwiches to the school picnic. If 38 students are in Mr. Brown's class, how many sandwiches are donated?

_____

Division of Whole Numbers

EXAMPLE   Write the problem in standard form. Divide.

168 ÷ 6 = _____28_____

$$\begin{array}{r} 28 \\ 6\overline{)168} \\ -12 \\ \hline 48 \\ -48 \\ \hline 0 \end{array}$$

Directions Rewrite the following division problems in the standard form and divide.

1. 128 ÷ 4 = _____

2. 477 ÷ 9 = _____

3. 266 ÷ 7 = _____

4. 480 ÷ 5 = _____

5. 824 ÷ 8 = _____

6. 864 ÷ 4 = _____

7. 1,290 ÷ 10 = _____

8. 1,771 ÷ 7 = _____

9. 1,008 ÷ 9 = _____

10. 3,069 ÷ 9 = _____

11. 948 ÷ 12 = _____

12. 1,472 ÷ 16 = _____

13. 1,360 ÷ 16 = _____

14. 2,160 ÷ 12 = _____

15. 3,036 ÷ 6 = _____

16. 8,844 ÷ 11 = _____

17. 6,030 ÷ 3 = _____

18. 5,400 ÷ 6 = _____

19. 1,710 ÷ 6 = _____

20. 1,820 ÷ 13 = _____

21. 14,910 ÷ 21 = _____

22. 15,625 ÷ 25 = _____

23. 12,720 ÷ 12 = _____

24. 13,797 ÷ 27 = _____

25. 27,060 ÷ 60 = _____

26. 21,350 ÷ 35 = _____

27. 11,216 ÷ 16 = _____

28. 12,030 ÷ 30 = _____

Directions Solve these word problems with division.

29. The Jiffy Messenger Service travels a total of 2,954 miles in one 7-day week. How many miles do the messengers average each day? _____

30. Marvin collects 1,170 bottle tops over a 45-day period. How many bottle tops does he average per day? _____

More Division of Whole Numbers

EXAMPLE Write the problem in standard form.
1,333 ÷ 9 = _____   Divide.

Express the remainder as a fraction.
Write the remainder over the divisor.

$$\begin{array}{r} 148\frac{1}{9} \\ 9\overline{)1,333} \\ -\underline{9} \\ 43 \\ -\underline{36} \\ 73 \\ -\underline{72} \\ 1 \end{array}$$

Directions Rewrite the following division problems in the standard form and divide. Express the remainders in fractional form.

1. 1,237 ÷ 6 = _____
2. 898 ÷ 6 = _____
3. 415 ÷ 6 = _____
4. 2,115 ÷ 11 = _____
5. 749 ÷ 6 = _____
6. 1,218 ÷ 12 = _____
7. 863 ÷ 7 = _____
8. 3,017 ÷ 15 = _____
9. 6,915 ÷ 4 = _____
10. 812 ÷ 82 = _____
11. 1,367 ÷ 17 = _____
12. 3,575 ÷ 28 = _____
13. 1,992 ÷ 10 = _____
14. 2,115 ÷ 63 = _____

15. 8,175 ÷ 35 = _____
16. 7,167 ÷ 20 = _____
17. 9,063 ÷ 75 = _____
18. 10,613 ÷ 53 = _____
19. 8,891 ÷ 22 = _____
20. 7,776 ÷ 78 = _____
21. 3,820 ÷ 45 = _____
22. 29,666 ÷ 30 = _____
23. 6,770 ÷ 65 = _____
24. 41,080 ÷ 80 = _____
25. 12,161 ÷ 11 = _____
26. 58,775 ÷ 40 = _____
27. 23,815 ÷ 15 = _____
28. 91,090 ÷ 90 = _____

Directions Solve these word problems with division. Express remainders in fractional form.

29. Maija's mother owned her car for 9 years, driving a total of 136,910 miles. Find the average number of miles driven per year. _____

30. Daniel drove his car 816 miles using 22 gallons of gas. Compute Daniel's gas mileage by dividing the number of miles driven by the number of gallons used. _____

Dividing Numbers by Powers of Ten

EXAMPLE   Write the problem in standard form and divide.

$480 \div 10 =$

Or move the decimal point one place to the left
for each zero in the divisor.

$48.0 \div 10 =$

$$
\begin{array}{r}
48 \\
10)\overline{480} \\
-\,40 \\
\hline
80 \\
-\,80 \\
\hline
0
\end{array}
$$

Directions Divide by these powers of ten.

1. $840 \div 10 =$ _____

2. $65,000 \div 100 =$ _____

3. $2,000 \div 100 =$ _____

4. $4,630 \div 10 =$ _____

5. $9,600 \div 100 =$ _____

6. $140,000 \div 1,000 =$ _____

7. $191,000 \div 10 =$ _____

8. $920,000 \div 100 =$ _____

9. $62,000 \div 100 =$ _____

10. $35,600 \div 100 =$ _____

11. $385,000 \div 100 =$ _____

12. $25,000,000 \div 1,000 =$ _____

13. $4,000,000 \div 1,000 =$ _____

14. $806,000 \div 10 =$ _____

15. $962,000 \div 100 =$ _____

16. $305,000 \div 100 =$ _____

17. $1,800,000 \div 1,000 =$ _____

18. $600,000 \div 1,000 =$ _____

19. $581,000 \div 10 =$ _____

20. $720,600 \div 100 =$ _____

21. $451,000 \div 1,000 =$ _____

22. $390,000 \div 10 =$ _____

23. $680,000 \div 100 =$ _____

24. $4,060,300 \div 10 =$ _____

25. $19,600 \div 10 =$ _____

26. $9,603,000 \div 1,000 =$ _____

27. $5,000,000 \div 100 =$ _____

28. $7,000,000 \div 10 =$ _____

29. $8,000,000 \div 100 =$ _____

30. $123,000 \div 1,000 =$ _____

31. $96,000,000 \div 1,000 =$ _____

32. $43,000 \div 1,000 =$ _____

33. $43,070,600 \div 10 =$ _____

34. $8,000,000 \div 10,000 =$ _____

35. $902,000 \div 100 =$ _____

36. $304,000,000 \div 100 =$ _____

37. $201,111,000 \div 10 =$ _____

38. $76,000,000 \div 1,000 =$ _____

39. $50,000 \div 10,000 =$ _____

40. $240,000 \div 10,000 =$ _____

Basic Operations with Whole Numbers

EXAMPLES

Add.   2 2
354
356
765
+ 87
1,562

Subtract.   1 12 9 14
2,304
− 567
1,737

Multiply.
23
× 44
092
+ 92
1,012

Divide.   1,145
3)3,435
− 3
0
4
− 3
13
− 12
15
− 15

Directions Add.

1. 243 + 321 + 132 + 68 =

2. 5,067 + 23 + 505 + 40 =

3. 1,102 + 705 + 4,033 =

4. 5,122 + 567 + 504 + 3,402 =

5. 30,304 + 4,030 + 20,300 + 1,102 =

6. 203,340 + 94,059 + 304,450 =

7. 2,000 + 90,089 + 50,481 =

8. 10,223 + 4,055 + 506 + 8,690 =

Directions Subtract.

9. 2,304 − 567 =

10. 304,119 − 4,053 =

11. 30,400 − 19,234 =

12. 102,556 − 9,806 =

13. 134,505 − 5,968 =

14. 900,800 − 203,788 =

15. 6,578,009 − 456,801 =

16. 340,599 − 9,875 =

Directions Multiply.

17. 23 × 44 =

18. 304 × 32 =

19. 579 × 23 =

20. 3,011 × 44 =

21. 4,503 × 23 =

22. 4,053 × 206 =

23. 5,098 × 2,304 =

24. 40,577 × 3,092 =

Directions Divide. Write the remainders in the fractional form.

25. 3,435 ÷ 3 =

26. 2,034 ÷ 9 =

27. 49,571 ÷ 9 =

28. 30,455 ÷ 5 =

29. 46,570 ÷ 45 =

30. 30,575 ÷ 25 =

Averages

EXAMPLE   Find the average of these numbers: 25, 73, 80, 73, 33, 95

Step 1 Add.

```
        25
        73
        80
        73
        33
     +  95
       379
```

Step 2 Divide.

```
    63.16 ≈ 63.2
6) 379.00
   – 36
     19
   – 18
     1 0
     – 6
       40
     – 36
```

Directions Compute the averages for the sets of numbers. Round to the nearest tenth.

1. 14, 12, 15, 11, 12, 13 _____

2. 83, 78, 53, 92, 67, 27 _____

3. 20, 28, 19, 31, 22, 18, 17, 30 _____

4. 78, 98, 77, 67, 75, 90, 80, 90, 80, 75, 70 _____

5. 30, 31, 37, 33, 38, 35, 32, 39, 34, 36 _____

6. 44, 46, 64, 66, 62, 69, 41, 40 _____

7. 103, 110, 152, 173, 177, 100, 150, 175, 152 _____

8. 205, 273, 198, 350, 220, 180, 280, 220 _____

9. 58, 74, 47, 83, 65, 36, 45, 46, 70, 53, 55, 38 _____

10. 163, 219, 300, 512, 375, 602, 735, 638, 881 _____

11. 3,004, 3,210, 3,387, 3,652, 3,470, 3,521, 3,980, 3,922 _____

12. 5,738, 5,755, 5,746, 5,789, 5,736, 5,725, 5,756, 5,731 _____

13. 230, 310, 222, 725, 600, 390, 512, 525, 510, 400, 500, 683 _____

14. 3,021, 5,361, 2,630, 6,110, 4,002, 3,006, 4,102, 4,120, 4,972, 3,500, 2,310 _____

15. 4,589, 4,530, 4,520, 4,500, 4,530, 4,528, 4,501, 4,554 _____

16. 7,800, 7,853, 7,835, 7,850, 7,812, 7,856, 7,851, 7,820 _____

17. 35, 78, 95, 83, 62, 89, 35, 60, 40, 66, 10, 31, 62, 89, 95 _____

18. 1,239, 1,264, 1,220, 1,250, 1,235, 1,260, 1,285, 1,240, 1,200, 1,290, 1,206 _____

Directions Solve these word problems by computing the average. Round the answers to the nearest tenth.

19. Deborah works as a part-time car mechanic. She works 26 hours her first week. What is her average number of hours worked per day for four days? _____

20. The band sells 523 tickets to its annual concert. There are 13 ticket sellers. Find the average number of tickets sold by each seller. _____

Exponents

EXAMPLE Read the number. Change the number into a problem and write the amount.

$$2^3 = 2 \times 2 \times 2 = \underline{\quad 8 \quad}$$

Directions Express the following without exponents.

1. $3^2 =$ _____	**21.** $20^3 =$ _____	**41.** $4^5 =$ _____
2. $4^2 =$ _____	**22.** $3^2 =$ _____	**42.** $21^2 =$ _____
3. $5^3 =$ _____	**23.** $5^4 =$ _____	**43.** $3^3 =$ _____
4. $4^3 =$ _____	**24.** $12^2 =$ _____	**44.** $10^6 =$ _____
5. $6^2 =$ _____	**25.** $10^3 =$ _____	**45.** $23^2 =$ _____
6. $10^2 =$ _____	**26.** $3^5 =$ _____	**46.** $14^2 =$ _____
7. $8^2 =$ _____	**27.** $22^3 =$ _____	**47.** $50^2 =$ _____
8. $2^5 =$ _____	**28.** $17^2 =$ _____	**48.** $100^2 =$ _____
9. $9^3 =$ _____	**29.** $15^2 =$ _____	**49.** $19^2 =$ _____
10. $5^2 =$ _____	**30.** $10^4 =$ _____	**50.** $33^2 =$ _____
11. $4^4 =$ _____	**31.** $12^3 =$ _____	**51.** $13^3 =$ _____
12. $2^4 =$ _____	**32.** $13^2 =$ _____	**52.** $16^2 =$ _____
13. $8^3 =$ _____	**33.** $20^2 =$ _____	**53.** $25^3 =$ _____
14. $9^2 =$ _____	**34.** $25^2 =$ _____	**54.** $17^3 =$ _____
15. $7^2 =$ _____	**35.** $15^3 =$ _____	**55.** $14^3 =$ _____
16. $10^5 =$ _____	**36.** $22^2 =$ _____	**56.** $5^5 =$ _____
17. $3^4 =$ _____	**37.** $11^3 =$ _____	**57.** $10^7 =$ _____
18. $6^3 =$ _____	**38.** $6^4 =$ _____	**58.** $11^4 =$ _____
19. $7^3 =$ _____	**39.** $2^6 =$ _____	**59.** $12^4 =$ _____
20. $11^2 =$ _____	**40.** $18^2 =$ _____	**60.** $10^9 =$ _____

Order of Operations

EXAMPLE   Follow the order of operations. $2 + 4 \times 2 =$ _____

$2 + \quad 8 \quad = \quad \underline{10}$

Directions Find the answers. Perform the operations in the correct order.

1. $3 + 5 \times 6 =$ _____

2. $3 \times 4 + 6 - 4 =$ _____

3. $4 \times 8 + 16 \div 2 =$ _____

4. $5 \times 2 - 6 \div 2 =$ _____

5. $4^2 \times 2 + 5 - 32 =$ _____

6. $3 \times 2 \times 2^3 - 4^2 =$ _____

7. $7 + 6 \times 2 - 2 + 2^3 =$ _____

8. $18 - 2 \times 4^2 \div 4 =$ _____

9. $10 + 8 \times 6 \div 12 - 2 =$ _____

10. $13 - 4 \times 5 \div 2 + 10 =$ _____

11. $15 \times 3 - 5^2 + 10 =$ _____

12. $7^2 + 2^4 - 2^3 =$ _____

13. $4 + 17 - 3 \times 7 =$ _____

14. $12^2 - 10^2 + 5 \times 2 =$ _____

15. $10^2 - 2 \times 4 + 3^2 =$ _____

16. $11^2 + 23 - 2^3 + 9 =$ _____

17. $20 - 12 \div 6 \times 3 =$ _____

18. $4^3 - 3 \times 12 \div 6 =$ _____

19. $15 + 4 - 11 + 2^5 =$ _____

20. $12 \times 2 \div 3 \times 2 + 3 =$ _____

21. $8 \times 6 \div 4 - 12 \div 6 =$ _____

22. $2^3 \times 3 \div 6 + 12 - 3 =$ _____

23. $45 \div 15 + 10 - 2^3 =$ _____

24. $15 \div 3 - 5 + 10^2 =$ _____

25. $12^2 \div 6 - 20 + 7 =$ _____

26. $8^2 + 9 \times 3 - 10 =$ _____

27. $18 \div 3^2 - 2 + 5^2 =$ _____

28. $5^3 \div 5 - 10 + 2^3 =$ _____

29. $81 \div 3^2 - 6 + 12 \div 2 =$ _____

30. $3 \times 6 \div 2 - 5 + 7 =$ _____

31. $10^2 \div 5^2 + 5 \times 6 \div 2 =$ _____

32. $25 \div 5^2 \times 5 + 5 - 10 =$ _____

33. $100 \div 10 \times 2^2 + 8 =$ _____

34. $18 - 9 \times 2 \div 3 + 3^2 =$ _____

35. $50 - 40 + 4 \times 7 =$ _____

36. $28 \div 4 \times 6 - 20 =$ _____

37. $3^3 \times 2^2 + 20 \div 2 =$ _____

38. $6^2 \times 3 \div 2 - 4^2 =$ _____

39. $14 \div 2 \times 3 - 21 =$ _____

40. $16 \times 2 \div 4 - 2 + 10 =$ _____

Factors

EXAMPLE   Factor the number.   Choose the correct factors.

F_{15} 1 × 15   **a.** 1, 5, 10, 15
         3 × 5   **b.** 1, 2, 3, 5
                  c. 1, 3, 5, 15
                  d. 1, 3, 6, 12

Directions Circle the answer that has the correct factors.

1. 24
a. 1, 2, 4, 6, 8, 12, 14
b. 1, 2, 4, 10, 12, 24
c. 1, 2, 3, 4, 6, 8, 12, 24
d. 2, 4, 6, 8, 10, 12, 24

2. 16
a. 1, 4, 8, 16
b. 1, 2, 4, 16
c. 1, 2, 4, 8, 16
d. 1, 2, 4, 8, 16, 32

3. 32
a. 1, 2, 8, 16, 32
b. 1, 2, 8, 16, 32, 64
c. 1, 2, 4, 8, 16, 32
d. 2, 4, 6, 8, 10, 32

4. 8
a. 2, 4, 8
b. 1, 2, 4, 8
c. 1, 2, 4, 8, 16
d. 1, 2, 4, 8, 12, 24

5. 10
a. 2, 5
b. 1, 2, 5, 10
c. 1, 2, 5, 10, 20
d. 1, 2, 5

6. 52
a. 1, 12, 24, 26, 30, 52
b. 26, 52
c. 1, 2, 4, 13, 26, 52
d. 1, 13, 15, 52

7. 14
a. 2, 7, 11, 14
b. 1, 2, 7, 14, 28
c. 2, 4, 7, 14
d. 1, 2, 7, 14

8. 42
a. 1, 6, 7, 12, 21, 42
b. 1, 2, 3, 6, 7, 14, 21, 42
c. 1, 6, 12, 42
d. 1, 2, 4, 12, 21, 42

9. 13
a. 1, 7, 13
b. 1, 13
c. 1, 7, 13, 26
d. 1, 2, 13, 19

10. 26
a. 1, 2, 20, 26
b. 1, 13, 26
c. 1, 2, 13, 26
d. 1, 26

11. 36
a. 2, 3, 4, 6, 8, 12, 24
b. 1, 2, 3, 4, 6, 9, 12, 18, 36
c. 1, 2, 4, 6, 8, 12, 36
d. 1, 3, 4, 6, 8, 12, 36

12. 12
a. 2, 3, 4, 6, 12
b. 3, 4, 6, 12, 24
c. 2, 4, 6, 24
d. 1, 2, 3, 4, 6, 12

13. 18
a. 1, 2, 3, 6, 9, 18
b. 1, 2, 3, 6, 9, 18, 32
c. 1, 2, 3, 6, 9, 18, 36
d. 1, 2, 3, 4, 6, 7, 18

14. 20
a. 2, 20
b. 2, 5, 10, 15, 20
c. 1, 2, 5, 10, 15, 20
d. 1, 2, 4, 5, 10, 20

15. 22
a. 1, 11, 22
b. 1, 11, 22, 44
c. 1, 2, 11, 22
d. 1, 22, 44

Multiples

$\boxed{\text{EXAMPLE}}$ M_4 Find the multiples of 4.

4×0	4×1	4×2	4×3	4×4
0	4	8	12	16

Choose the correct multiples.
a. 0, 1, 2, 4
b. 0, 4, 10, 12
c. 0, 1, 4, 8
d. 0, 4, 8, 12 (circled)

Directions Circle the answer that has the correct multiples. Note: Some multiples may be missing from a correct answer.

1. M_2
a. 2, 4, 6, 8, 11
b. 0, 4, 6, 8, 12
c. 0, 2, 4, 5, 6, 8
d. 0, 2, 3, 4, 5, 6

2. M_{11}
a. 0, 1, 11, 22, 121
b. 0, 11, 22, 33, 44, 56
c. 11, 22, 33, 111
d. 0, 11, 22, 33, 121

3. M_4
a. 0, 2, 4, 6, 8, 16
b. 4, 8, 16, 32, 36
c. 0, 4, 6, 8, 12, 20
d. 0, 14, 28, 56, 100

4. M_6
a. 0, 2, 4, 6, 8, 9
b. 0, 6, 12, 18, 24
c. 1, 6, 12, 18, 24
d. 1, 3, 6, 9, 18, 24

5. M_{30}
a. 0, 10, 30, 60, 90
b. 0, 30, 60, 90, 120
c. 0, 15, 30, 45, 60
d. 1, 15, 30, 40, 60

6. M_3
a. 0, 3, 5, 6, 9, 12
b. 3, 6, 9, 12, 14
c. 0, 3, 6, 12, 15
d. 1, 3, 6, 9, 12, 15

7. M_7
a. 0, 7, 14, 28, 56, 112
b. 0, 3, 7, 14, 28, 35
c. 0, 7, 11, 22, 33, 44
d. 1, 7, 14, 28, 35, 40

8. M_9
a. 0, 9, 18, 27, 36
b. 0, 9, 27, 38, 45
c. 0, 19, 38, 76
d. 0, 1, 2, 3, 4, 5

9. M_{20}
a. 0, 20, 40, 60, 80
b. 0, 20, 30, 40, 50
c. 1, 20, 40, 60, 80
d. 1, 10, 20, 30, 40

10. M_{40}
a. 0, 40, 80, 120, 160
b. 1, 40, 80, 120, 160
c. 1, 20, 40, 60, 80
d. 0, 20, 40, 60, 80

11. M_5
a. 0, 5, 10, 12, 15
b. 0, 10, 15, 20, 30
c. 1, 5, 10, 15, 20
d. 0, 10, 18, 20, 25

12. M_{10}
a. 0, 10, 15, 20, 25
b. 0, 5, 10, 15, 20
c. 10, 15, 20, 25, 30
d. 0, 10, 30, 50, 100

13. M_{12}
a. 0, 12, 24, 36, 44
b. 0, 12, 16, 24, 28
c. 0, 12, 24, 36, 48
d. 0, 10, 12, 14, 16

14. M_{13}
a. 13, 29, 39, 52
b. 0, 13, 23, 39
c. 1, 13, 26, 52
d. 0, 13, 26, 39

15. M_{50}
a. 1, 50, 100, 150
b. 0, 50, 100, 150
c. 1, 25, 50, 75
d. 0, 10, 15, 25

Prime and Composite Numbers

<table>
<tr><td>**EXAMPLE**</td><td>Identify all the factors of a number. F_9 = 1, 3, 9
Tell whether the number is a prime or composite number.
9 has three factors, so it is a composite number.</td></tr>
</table>

Directions Write *prime* or *composite* for each number given.

1. 23 _____	**19.** 21 _____	**37.** 12 _____
2. 25 _____	**20.** 44 _____	**38.** 7 _____
3. 45 _____	**21.** 17 _____	**39.** 58 _____
4. 19 _____	**22.** 26 _____	**40.** 98 _____
5. 84 _____	**23.** 102 _____	**41.** 62 _____
6. 29 _____	**24.** 77 _____	**42.** 60 _____
7. 73 _____	**25.** 42 _____	**43.** 22 _____
8. 37 _____	**26.** 54 _____	**44.** 49 _____
9. 55 _____	**27.** 4 _____	**45.** 31 _____
10. 78 _____	**28.** 100 _____	**46.** 1 _____
11. 15 _____	**29.** 27 _____	**47.** 400 _____
12. 220 _____	**30.** 79 _____	**48.** 2 _____
13. 110 _____	**31.** 55 _____	**49.** 3 _____
14. 6 _____	**32.** 204 _____	**50.** 300 _____
15. 120 _____	**33.** 41 _____	
16. 72 _____	**34.** 155 _____	
17. 350 _____	**35.** 29 _____	
18. 410 _____	**36.** 57 _____	

Sets of Numbers

EXAMPLE   Identify the set of even numbers. Even numbers are multiples of 2.

1, 2, 3, 5, 6, 8, 10, 12

Set of even numbers   2, 6, 8, 10, 12

Directions   Write the sets from the given numbers.

1, 2, 3, 4, 5, 6, 7, 8, 9, 10, 11, 12, 13, 14, 15, 16, 17, 18, 19, 20,

21, 22, 23, 24, 25, 26, 27, 28, 29, 30, 31, 32, 33, 34, 35, 36, 37,

38, 39, 40, 41, 42, 43, 44, 45, 46, 47, 48, 49, 50

1. The set of even numbers

_____

2. The set of odd numbers

_____

3. The set of prime numbers

_____

4. The set of numbers that will divide into 100 with zero as a remainder

_____

5. The set of numbers that is multiples of 3   _____

6. The set of numbers that is multiples of 6   _____

7. The set of numbers that is multiples of 10   _____

8. The set of numbers that is multiples of 100   _____

9. The set of numbers that is factors of 100   _____

10. The set of numbers that is factors of 20   _____

11. The set of numbers that is factors of 10   _____

12. The set of numbers that is factors of 8   _____

13. The set of numbers that is factors of 6   _____

14. The set of numbers that is factors of 30   _____

15. The set of numbers that is factors of 12   _____

Prime Numbers

EXAMPLE   List prime numbers from the given set.
     2, 3, 4, 5

Identify prime numbers, which are numbers that have exactly 2 factors.
     2 has 2 factors
     3 has 2 factors
     4 has 3 factors
     5 has 2 factors
Prime numbers are 2, 3, 5.

Directions   Write the sets from the given numbers.

1, 2, 3, 4, 5, 6, 7, 8, 9, 10, 11, 12, 13, 14, 15, 16, 17, 18, 19, 20,

21, 22, 23, 24, 25, 26, 27, 28, 29, 30, 31, 32, 33, 34, 35, 36, 37,

38, 39, 40, 41, 42, 43, 44, 45

1. List the prime numbers in order from smallest to largest from the set given.

_____

2. List the even numbers in order from smallest to largest from the set given.

_____

3. List the odd numbers in order from smallest to largest from the set given.

_____

4. Add pairs of prime numbers. Exclude 2 from your additions.

Can you predict an odd or even answer? _____ Summarize your results.

_____

5. Add pairs of odd numbers. Can you predict an odd or even answer? _____
Summarize your results.

_____

6. Add pairs of even numbers. Can you predict an odd or even answer? _____
Summarize your results.

_____

Find the three prime addends for each of the following numbers.

7. 12 = _____   **9.** 14 = _____

8. 19 = _____   **10.** 21 = _____

Divisibility Tests

  Use the divisibility test to determine if this number is divisible by 3.

     123   Add the digits.   1 + 2 + 3 = 6

Determine if the sum is a multiple of 3. 6 is a multiple of 3.
     123 is divisible by 3.

Directions Perform the divisibility test to complete the chart.
           Write *Yes* or *No* for each space.

Number	Divisible by 2?	Divisible by 3?	Divisible by 5?
1. 12,034			
2. 31,241			
3. 21,453			
4. 3,040,511			
5. 989,798			
6. 10,233			
7. 20,394			
8. 3,012,211			
9. 50,321			
10. 293,100			

Number	Divisible by 4?	Divisible by 9?	Divisible by 10?
11. 20,349			
12. 13,536			
13. 12,350			
14. 182,340			
15. 125,350			
16. 30,451			
17. 10,800			
18. 100,237			
19. 584,750			
20. 95,832			

Prime Factorization

EXAMPLES
Complete factor trees to find prime factorization.

Find prime factors for 45 and 34.

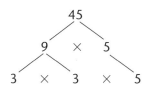

Directions Complete factor trees for these numbers.

1. 48   **4.** 36   **7.** 39   **9.** 72

2. 44   **5.** 32   **8.** 38   **10.** 52

3. 64   **6.** 28

Least Common Multiple

EXAMPLE   Find the LCM (12, 6).

M_{12} = 12, 24, 36

M_6 = 6, 12, 18, 24

LCM (12, 6) = 12

Directions Find the least common multiple and show the steps.

1. Find the LCM (10, 15).

_____

_____

_____

2. Find the LCM (12, 16).

_____

_____

_____

3. Find the LCM (3, 8).

_____

_____

_____

4. Find the LCM (8, 9).

_____

_____

_____

5. Find the LCM (3, 7).

_____

_____

_____

6. Find the LCM (36, 12).

_____

_____

_____

7. Find the LCM (7, 6).

_____

_____

_____

8. Find the LCM (5, 8).

_____

_____

_____

9. Find the LCM (4, 6).

_____

_____

_____

10. Find the LCM (5, 7).

_____

_____

_____

Least Common Multiple/Greatest Common Factor

EXAMPLES Find the factors. Underline greatest common numbers in both sets.

LCM (3, 5)   GCF (10, 25)

M_3 = {0, 3, 9, 12, <u>15</u>, . . .} F_{10} = {1, 2, <u>5</u>, 10}

M_5 = {0, 5, 10, <u>15</u>, 20, . . .} F_{25} = {1, <u>5</u>, 25}

LCM (3, 5) = 15   GCF = 5

Directions Find the least common multiple and show the steps.

1. Find the LCM (11, 33).   **3.** Find the LCM (15, 12).

_____   _____

_____   _____

_____   _____

2. Find the LCM (5, 16).   **4.** Find the LCM (12, 10).

_____   _____

_____   _____

_____   _____

Directions Find the greatest common factor.

5. GCF (18, 16) _____   **11.** GCF (12, 20) _____

6. GCF (8, 36) _____   **12.** GCF (32, 36) _____

7. GCF (12, 15) _____   **13.** GCF (12, 16) _____

8. GCF (6, 26) _____   **14.** GCF (20, 8) _____

9. GCF (18, 4) _____   **15.** GCF (20, 15) _____

10. GCF (14, 4) _____

Using Prime Factorization

EXAMPLES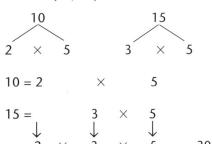

LCM   (10, 15)   GCF   (10, 15)

Directions Find the least common multiple (LCM) for these pairs of numbers.

1. Find the LCM (25, 15).   **3.** Find the LCM (16, 18).

2. Find the LCM (5, 12).   **4.** Find the LCM (27, 9).

Directions Find the greatest common factor (GCF) for each pair of numbers.

5. GCF (10, 25)   **8.** GCF (14, 8)

6. GCF (20, 30)   **9.** GCF (22, 55)

7. GCF (22, 77)   **10.** GCF (44, 48)

Comparing Fractions

Directions Compare the fractions in each pair. Use < or > for each pair.

1. $\frac{3}{5}$ $\frac{4}{7}$

2. $\frac{5}{6}$ $\frac{7}{8}$

3. $\frac{5}{7}$ $\frac{7}{8}$

4. $\frac{2}{5}$ $\frac{4}{1}$

5. $\frac{3}{13}$ $\frac{6}{20}$

6. $\frac{3}{8}$ $\frac{9}{20}$

7. $\frac{6}{11}$ $\frac{5}{9}$

8. $\frac{5}{8}$ $\frac{10}{17}$

9. $\frac{1}{2}$ $\frac{5}{11}$

10. $\frac{2}{13}$ $\frac{4}{15}$

11. $\frac{15}{16}$ $\frac{16}{17}$

12. $\frac{2}{13}$ $\frac{3}{14}$

13. $\frac{1}{8}$ $\frac{2}{13}$

14. $\frac{5}{21}$ $\frac{18}{31}$

15. $\frac{2}{15}$ $\frac{6}{21}$

16. $\frac{7}{13}$ $\frac{6}{32}$

17. $\frac{1}{5}$ $\frac{1}{9}$

18. $\frac{2}{21}$ $\frac{3}{31}$

19. $\frac{1}{3}$ $\frac{2}{7}$

20. $\frac{6}{7}$ $\frac{8}{1}$

21. $\frac{3}{5}$ $\frac{1}{2}$

22. $\frac{2}{8}$ $\frac{4}{17}$

23. $\frac{6}{10}$ $\frac{1}{5}$

24. $\frac{5}{10}$ $\frac{10}{21}$

25. $\frac{4}{7}$ $\frac{5}{11}$

26. $\frac{3}{5}$ $\frac{6}{11}$

27. $\frac{4}{5}$ $\frac{2}{20}$

28. $\frac{6}{11}$ $\frac{5}{22}$

29. $\frac{1}{2}$ $\frac{2}{8}$

30. $\frac{4}{11}$ $\frac{8}{21}$

31. $\frac{9}{10}$ $\frac{4}{5}$

32. $\frac{7}{12}$ $\frac{7}{10}$

33. $\frac{6}{9}$ $\frac{12}{17}$

34. $\frac{4}{12}$ $\frac{2}{7}$

35. $\frac{3}{13}$ $\frac{1}{6}$

36. $\frac{8}{15}$ $\frac{15}{16}$

37. $\frac{3}{8}$ $\frac{5}{13}$

38. $\frac{10}{12}$ $\frac{14}{16}$

39. $\frac{2}{6}$ $\frac{4}{14}$

40. $\frac{1}{12}$ $\frac{4}{24}$

41. $\frac{6}{11}$ $\frac{5}{13}$

42. $\frac{2}{4}$ $\frac{10}{22}$

43. $\frac{8}{10}$ $\frac{4}{40}$

44. $\frac{6}{7}$ $\frac{18}{20}$

45. $\frac{4}{6}$ $\frac{8}{10}$

46. $\frac{6}{10}$ $\frac{2}{4}$

47. $\frac{11}{23}$ $\frac{22}{31}$

48. $\frac{9}{15}$ $\frac{18}{31}$

49. $\frac{10}{11}$ $\frac{20}{23}$

50. $\frac{4}{8}$ $\frac{5}{11}$

51. $\frac{10}{23}$ $\frac{15}{32}$

52. $\frac{11}{13}$ $\frac{5}{17}$

53. $\frac{9}{10}$ $\frac{13}{14}$

54. $\frac{7}{11}$ $\frac{8}{12}$

55. $\frac{3}{7}$ $\frac{5}{9}$

56. $\frac{5}{6}$ $\frac{16}{17}$

57. $\frac{2}{11}$ $\frac{2}{3}$

58. $\frac{1}{8}$ $\frac{5}{45}$

59. $\frac{13}{20}$ $\frac{1}{5}$

60. $\frac{7}{10}$ $\frac{6}{15}$

Working with Fractions

EXAMPLE Divide to find out how many times one denominator goes into the other.
Multiply the numerator by the quotient.

$\frac{2}{5} = \frac{}{25}$ Divide 25 by 5. $25 \div 5 = 5$

$\frac{2}{5} \times \frac{5}{5} = \frac{10}{25}$

$\frac{2}{5} = \frac{10}{25}$

Directions Express these fractions in higher terms.

1. $\frac{3}{5} = \frac{}{50}$
2. $\frac{1}{3} = \frac{}{18}$
3. $\frac{5}{6} = \frac{}{24}$
4. $\frac{7}{8} = \frac{}{32}$
5. $\frac{7}{8} = \frac{}{56}$
6. $\frac{3}{7} = \frac{}{21}$
7. $\frac{2}{9} = \frac{}{36}$
8. $\frac{1}{5} = \frac{}{30}$
9. $\frac{1}{4} = \frac{}{20}$
10. $\frac{5}{11} = \frac{}{121}$
11. $\frac{4}{9} = \frac{}{72}$
12. $\frac{3}{11} = \frac{}{44}$
13. $\frac{2}{3} = \frac{}{18}$
14. $\frac{7}{10} = \frac{}{80}$
15. $\frac{3}{4} = \frac{}{16}$

16. $\frac{6}{7} = \frac{}{42}$
17. $\frac{7}{13} = \frac{}{39}$
18. $\frac{5}{8} = \frac{}{64}$
19. $\frac{2}{13} = \frac{}{52}$
20. $\frac{1}{9} = \frac{}{99}$
21. $\frac{11}{12} = \frac{}{60}$
22. $\frac{8}{15} = \frac{}{45}$
23. $\frac{6}{19} = \frac{}{76}$
24. $\frac{4}{7} = \frac{}{63}$
25. $\frac{13}{15} = \frac{}{105}$
26. $\frac{8}{17} = \frac{}{34}$
27. $\frac{10}{19} = \frac{}{38}$
28. $\frac{1}{13} = \frac{}{65}$
29. $\frac{10}{11} = \frac{}{55}$
30. $\frac{15}{16} = \frac{}{64}$

31. $\frac{5}{14} = \frac{}{56}$
32. $\frac{2}{23} = \frac{}{92}$
33. $\frac{5}{7} = \frac{}{210}$
34. $\frac{4}{13} = \frac{}{39}$
35. $\frac{5}{10} = \frac{}{1,000}$
36. $\frac{9}{17} = \frac{}{51}$
37. $\frac{4}{11} = \frac{}{99}$
38. $\frac{23}{30} = \frac{}{90}$
39. $\frac{3}{7} = \frac{}{84}$
40. $\frac{3}{16} = \frac{}{80}$
41. $\frac{12}{15} = \frac{}{60}$
42. $\frac{5}{6} = \frac{}{54}$
43. $\frac{8}{14} = \frac{}{42}$
44. $\frac{18}{23} = \frac{}{92}$
45. $\frac{9}{22} = \frac{}{220}$

46. $\frac{5}{8} = \frac{}{96}$
47. $\frac{5}{21} = \frac{}{105}$
48. $\frac{5}{32} = \frac{}{160}$
49. $\frac{6}{38} = \frac{}{380}$
50. $\frac{35}{70} = \frac{}{280}$
51. $\frac{6}{30} = \frac{}{390}$
52. $\frac{3}{13} = \frac{}{65}$
53. $\frac{5}{11} = \frac{}{121}$
54. $\frac{45}{60} = \frac{}{480}$
55. $\frac{15}{18} = \frac{}{72}$
56. $\frac{8}{52} = \frac{}{156}$
57. $\frac{6}{16} = \frac{}{80}$
58. $\frac{7}{12} = \frac{}{156}$
59. $\frac{9}{29} = \frac{}{145}$
60. $\frac{5}{21} = \frac{}{126}$

Renaming Fractions

Rename fractions by expressing them in lowest terms.
Divide the numerator and denominator by their greatest common factor.

$$\frac{10}{14} = \frac{10 \div 2}{14 \div 2} = \frac{5}{7}$$

Directions Express these fractions and mixed numbers in their lowest terms.

1. $\frac{9}{15} =$ _____

2. $\frac{9}{27} =$ _____

3. $\frac{18}{22} =$ _____

4. $13\frac{10}{15} =$ _____

5. $2\frac{12}{14} =$ _____

6. $\frac{10}{20} =$ _____

7. $\frac{13}{39} =$ _____

8. $\frac{28}{40} =$ _____

9. $\frac{10}{50} =$ _____

10. $6\frac{5}{40} =$ _____

11. $13\frac{70}{80} =$ _____

12. $27\frac{52}{104} =$ _____

13. $\frac{30}{33} =$ _____

14. $9\frac{24}{46} =$ _____

15. $\frac{9}{21} =$ _____

16. $\frac{150}{200} =$ _____

17. $20\frac{18}{57} =$ _____

18. $\frac{46}{52} =$ _____

19. $\frac{28}{120} =$ _____

20. $\frac{102}{128} =$ _____

21. $\frac{178}{220} =$ _____

22. $8\frac{23}{92} =$ _____

23. $51\frac{66}{121} =$ _____

24. $9\frac{15}{33} =$ _____

25. $\frac{44}{108} =$ _____

26. $9\frac{31}{62} =$ _____

27. $6\frac{7}{63} =$ _____

28. $\frac{16}{64} =$ _____

29. $\frac{88}{121} =$ _____

30. $\frac{58}{64} =$ _____

31. $11\frac{62}{92} =$ _____

32. $18\frac{35}{225} =$ _____

33. $\frac{28}{54} =$ _____

34. $\frac{20}{55} =$ _____

35. $\frac{36}{38} =$ _____

36. $\frac{42}{150} =$ _____

37. $\frac{20}{25} =$ _____

38. $\frac{11}{88} =$ _____

39. $\frac{33}{39} =$ _____

40. $\frac{88}{112} =$ _____

41. $\frac{38}{56} =$ _____

42. $\frac{15}{54} =$ _____

43. $\frac{56}{108} =$ _____

44. $\frac{38}{106} =$ _____

45. $\frac{25}{155} =$ _____

46. $\frac{18}{450} =$ _____

47. $\frac{210}{280} =$ _____

48. $\frac{64}{160} =$ _____

49. $\frac{30}{72} =$ _____

50. $\frac{450}{480} =$ _____

51. $\frac{22}{42} =$ _____

52. $\frac{140}{280} =$ _____

53. $\frac{150}{300} =$ _____

54. $\frac{84}{96} =$ _____

55. $\frac{50}{68} =$ _____

56. $\frac{78}{104} =$ _____

57. $\frac{41}{205} =$ _____

58. $\frac{69}{207} =$ _____

59. $\frac{42}{122} =$ _____

60. $\frac{55}{300} =$ _____

Mixed Numbers

EXAMPLE   Rename $1\frac{2}{3}$ as an improper fraction $3 \times 1 = 3$ $3 + 2 = 5$ $1\frac{2}{3} = \frac{5}{3}$

Multiply the whole number by the denominator. Then, add the numerator.
Write the new numerator over the same denominator.

Directions   Rename these mixed numbers as improper fractions.

1. $2\frac{1}{6} =$ _____

2. $1\frac{1}{2} =$ _____

3. $2\frac{1}{5} =$ _____

4. $1\frac{5}{6} =$ _____

5. $4\frac{1}{5} =$ _____

6. $3\frac{2}{5} =$ _____

7. $1\frac{1}{6} =$ _____

8. $9\frac{2}{7} =$ _____

9. $4\frac{3}{4} =$ _____

10. $2\frac{5}{11} =$ _____

11. $1\frac{5}{9} =$ _____

12. $13\frac{2}{7} =$ _____

13. $20\frac{1}{2} =$ _____

14. $6\frac{2}{9} =$ _____

15. $3\frac{4}{7} =$ _____

16. $2\frac{2}{3} =$ _____

17. $15\frac{1}{3} =$ _____

18. $6\frac{4}{11} =$ _____

19. $15\frac{3}{4} =$ _____

20. $6\frac{2}{5} =$ _____

21. $7\frac{1}{5} =$ _____

22. $33\frac{2}{3} =$ _____

23. $17\frac{1}{2} =$ _____

24. $2\frac{2}{17} =$ _____

25. $9\frac{5}{11} =$ _____

26. $8\frac{5}{13} =$ _____

27. $18\frac{3}{5} =$ _____

28. $3\frac{2}{19} =$ _____

29. $9\frac{10}{11} =$ _____

30. $2\frac{13}{14} =$ _____

31. $3\frac{16}{17} =$ _____

32. $4\frac{2}{19} =$ _____

33. $5\frac{7}{9} =$ _____

34. $5\frac{2}{12} =$ _____

35. $6\frac{3}{13} =$ _____

36. $4\frac{1}{13} =$ _____

37. $7\frac{10}{11} =$ _____

38. $8\frac{13}{15} =$ _____

39. $1\frac{7}{22} =$ _____

40. $3\frac{5}{11} =$ _____

41. $4\frac{5}{20} =$ _____

42. $2\frac{3}{22} =$ _____

43. $5\frac{11}{16} =$ _____

44. $21\frac{2}{61} =$ _____

45. $5\frac{13}{20} =$ _____

46. $7\frac{20}{23} =$ _____

47. $5\frac{5}{60} =$ _____

48. $1\frac{2}{13} =$ _____

49. $3\frac{5}{11} =$ _____

50. $7\frac{2}{25} =$ _____

51. $4\frac{3}{29} =$ _____

52. $4\frac{2}{32} =$ _____

53. $1\frac{7}{18} =$ _____

54. $11\frac{5}{11} =$ _____

55. $20\frac{1}{16} =$ _____

56. $10\frac{2}{17} =$ _____

57. $11\frac{5}{21} =$ _____

58. $5\frac{11}{12} =$ _____

59. $7\frac{2}{30} =$ _____

60. $2\frac{6}{23} =$ _____

Renaming Improper Fractions

EXAMPLE   Express the improper fractions as mixed numbers.
Divide the numerator by the denominator.
Simplify if necessary.

$$\frac{78}{9}$$

$$9)\overline{78}$$
$$\underline{-72}$$
$$6 \quad \text{remainder is 6}$$

Solution: $8\frac{6}{9}$ or $8\frac{2}{3}$

Directions Rename the improper fractions as mixed numbers.
Simplify if necessary.

1. $\frac{15}{7}$ = _____

2. $\frac{29}{6}$ = _____

3. $\frac{51}{30}$ = _____

4. $\frac{33}{8}$ = _____

5. $\frac{44}{10}$ = _____

6. $\frac{20}{10}$ = _____

7. $\frac{35}{2}$ = _____

8. $\frac{28}{8}$ = _____

9. $\frac{57}{8}$ = _____

10. $\frac{53}{23}$ = _____

11. $\frac{77}{10}$ = _____

12. $\frac{42}{13}$ = _____

13. $\frac{62}{11}$ = _____

14. $\frac{82}{11}$ = _____

15. $\frac{39}{11}$ = _____

16. $\frac{87}{33}$ = _____

17. $\frac{18}{11}$ = _____

18. $\frac{72}{18}$ = _____

19. $\frac{71}{14}$ = _____

20. $\frac{57}{13}$ = _____

21. $\frac{19}{10}$ = _____

22. $\frac{54}{20}$ = _____

23. $\frac{46}{20}$ = _____

24. $\frac{66}{11}$ = _____

25. $\frac{53}{10}$ = _____

26. $\frac{34}{12}$ = _____

27. $\frac{63}{8}$ = _____

28. $\frac{64}{9}$ = _____

29. $\frac{29}{18}$ = _____

30. $\frac{98}{9}$ = _____

Improper Fractions to Mixed Numbers

EXAMPLE   Rename $\frac{13}{5}$. Divide the numerator by the denominator.
Simplify if necessary.

$$5\overline{)13} \quad \frac{2\ \ \frac{3}{5}}{\begin{array}{r} 13 \\ -10 \\ \hline 3 \end{array}}$$

Directions   Rename these improper fractions as mixed numbers.
Simplify if necessary.

1. $\frac{14}{6}$ = _____

2. $\frac{16}{7}$ = _____

3. $\frac{28}{7}$ = _____

4. $\frac{15}{2}$ = _____

5. $\frac{33}{4}$ = _____

6. $\frac{18}{5}$ = _____

7. $\frac{25}{4}$ = _____

8. $\frac{62}{6}$ = _____

9. $\frac{30}{7}$ = _____

10. $\frac{35}{8}$ = _____

11. $\frac{18}{8}$ = _____

12. $\frac{30}{4}$ = _____

13. $\frac{75}{25}$ = _____

14. $\frac{72}{10}$ = _____

15. $\frac{26}{3}$ = _____

16. $\frac{72}{19}$ = _____

17. $\frac{60}{9}$ = _____

18. $\frac{120}{11}$ = _____

19. $\frac{36}{17}$ = _____

20. $\frac{57}{9}$ = _____

21. $\frac{39}{16}$ = _____

22. $\frac{37}{5}$ = _____

23. $\frac{17}{2}$ = _____

24. $\frac{60}{28}$ = _____

25. $\frac{33}{10}$ = _____

26. $\frac{135}{9}$ = _____

27. $\frac{200}{120}$ = _____

28. $\frac{25}{21}$ = _____

29. $\frac{63}{12}$ = _____

30. $\frac{130}{12}$ = _____

31. $\frac{38}{6}$ = _____

32. $\frac{17}{5}$ = _____

33. $\frac{18}{11}$ = _____

34. $\frac{23}{2}$ = _____

35. $\frac{54}{11}$ = _____

36. $\frac{92}{5}$ = _____

37. $\frac{36}{13}$ = _____

38. $\frac{39}{5}$ = _____

39. $\frac{51}{11}$ = _____

40. $\frac{46}{14}$ = _____

41. $\frac{22}{5}$ = _____

42. $\frac{87}{12}$ = _____

43. $\frac{57}{12}$ = _____

44. $\frac{62}{11}$ = _____

45. $\frac{73}{10}$ = _____

46. $\frac{91}{8}$ = _____

47. $\frac{76}{7}$ = _____

48. $\frac{89}{11}$ = _____

49. $\frac{48}{23}$ = _____

50. $\frac{98}{46}$ = _____

51. $\frac{88}{23}$ = _____

52. $\frac{105}{15}$ = _____

53. $\frac{28}{6}$ = _____

54. $\frac{100}{7}$ = _____

55. $\frac{49}{3}$ = _____

56. $\frac{65}{2}$ = _____

57. $\frac{85}{17}$ = _____

58. $\frac{59}{9}$ = _____

59. $\frac{99}{10}$ = _____

60. $\frac{46}{3}$ = _____

Multiplication of Fractions

EXAMPLE   Multiply numerators. Multiply denominators.
Simplify if necessary.

$$\frac{3}{5} \times \frac{7}{8} = \frac{3 \times 7}{5 \times 8} = \frac{21}{40}$$

Directions   Multiply these fractions. Simplify the answers to the lowest terms.

1. $\frac{1}{5} \times \frac{3}{4} =$ _____

2. $\frac{4}{5} \times \frac{10}{11} =$ _____

3. $\frac{6}{9} \times \frac{1}{3} =$ _____

4. $\frac{2}{5} \times \frac{4}{10} =$ _____

5. $8 \times \frac{6}{7} =$ _____

6. $\frac{7}{9} \times 1\frac{1}{2} =$ _____

7. $\frac{2}{9} \times 1\frac{1}{8} =$ _____

8. $\frac{3}{11} \times 3\frac{2}{3} =$ _____

9. $\frac{7}{13} \times \frac{13}{5} =$ _____

10. $\frac{8}{11} \times \frac{1}{5} =$ _____

11. $\frac{2}{5} \times \frac{2}{17} =$ _____

12. $\frac{5}{8} \times \frac{3}{8} =$ _____

13. $\frac{4}{6} \times \frac{2}{3} =$ _____

14. $\frac{1}{3} \times \frac{6}{10} =$ _____

15. $\frac{1}{2} \times \frac{3}{5} =$ _____

16. $\frac{35}{38} \times \frac{4}{5} =$ _____

17. $\frac{6}{11} \times 2\frac{5}{6} =$ _____

18. $\frac{7}{12} \times \frac{3}{7} =$ _____

19. $\frac{1}{6} \times \frac{2}{5} =$ _____

20. $\frac{2}{5} \times 2\frac{2}{5} =$ _____

21. $1\frac{3}{7} \times \frac{5}{8} =$ _____

22. $\frac{6}{13} \times 2\frac{1}{6} =$ _____

23. $3\frac{1}{5} \times \frac{3}{11} =$ _____

24. $4\frac{1}{5} \times 7 =$ _____

25. $5\frac{2}{5} \times 10 =$ _____

26. $5\frac{2}{13} \times \frac{1}{6} =$ _____

27. $3\frac{4}{5} \times 65 =$ _____

28. $2\frac{1}{4} \times 4 =$ _____

29. $2\frac{1}{5} \times 5\frac{1}{2} =$ _____

30. $7\frac{2}{5} \times 5\frac{2}{7} =$ _____

31. $2\frac{1}{20} \times 20\frac{5}{10} =$ _____

32. $5\frac{6}{13} \times 1\frac{1}{2} =$ _____

33. $7\frac{1}{5} \times \frac{65}{72} =$ _____

34. $5\frac{2}{7} \times 1\frac{1}{2} =$ _____

35. $7\frac{5}{8} \times 2\frac{3}{4} =$ _____

36. $5\frac{2}{12} \times 1\frac{1}{2} =$ _____

37. $5\frac{4}{11} \times 1\frac{1}{3} =$ _____

38. $3\frac{4}{5} \times 1\frac{1}{2} =$ _____

39. $8\frac{8}{9} \times \frac{18}{20} =$ _____

40. $3\frac{1}{5} \times 5\frac{1}{3} =$ _____

41. $3\frac{1}{3} \times \frac{1}{5} =$ _____

42. $2\frac{3}{7} \times \frac{14}{17} =$ _____

43. $3\frac{5}{6} \times \frac{12}{46} =$ _____

44. $5\frac{2}{7} \times 5 =$ _____

45. $7\frac{2}{5} \times 1\frac{1}{5} =$ _____

Multiplying Mixed Numbers

EXAMPLE   Change mixed numbers to improper fractions.
Multiply. Simplify if necessary.

$$2\frac{1}{5} \times \frac{1}{5} =$$

$$\frac{11}{5} \times \frac{1}{5} = \frac{11}{25}$$

Directions   Multiply these fractions.

1. $4\frac{2}{5} \times 1\frac{3}{5} =$

2. $1\frac{1}{6} \times 1\frac{2}{7} =$

3. $3\frac{1}{3} \times 1\frac{3}{5} =$

4. $\frac{3}{7} \times 1\frac{1}{5} =$

5. $\frac{1}{7} \times 2\frac{1}{4} =$

6. $1\frac{1}{13} \times 2\frac{3}{7} =$

7. $2\frac{1}{4} \times 2\frac{1}{3} =$

8. $1\frac{1}{3} \times 3\frac{1}{2} =$

9. $2\frac{2}{3} \times \frac{1}{6} =$

10. $1\frac{1}{3} \times 2\frac{2}{5} =$

11. $\frac{1}{5} \times 2\frac{1}{3} =$

12. $2\frac{5}{6} \times 1\frac{5}{7} =$

13. $2\frac{1}{3} \times 3\frac{1}{5} =$

14. $2\frac{2}{3} \times 3\frac{1}{3} =$

15. $\frac{3}{5} \times 3\frac{1}{3} =$

Dividing Fractions

EXAMPLE   Invert the divisor. Multiply. Simplify if necessary.

$$\frac{2}{5} \div \frac{3}{7} =$$

$$\frac{2}{5} \times \frac{7}{3} = \frac{14}{15}$$

Directions Divide these fractions. Remember to invert the divisor.
Show your work. See the example.

1. $\frac{3}{10} \div \frac{4}{5} =$

2. $\frac{13}{12} \div \frac{15}{18} =$

3. $\frac{5}{9} \div \frac{8}{12} =$

4. $\frac{7}{5} \div \frac{10}{15} =$

5. $\frac{4}{12} \div \frac{6}{8} =$

6. $\frac{8}{9} \div \frac{6}{7} =$

7. $\frac{5}{12} \div \frac{7}{8} =$

8. $\frac{7}{10} \div \frac{10}{15} =$

9. $\frac{2}{7} \div \frac{7}{8} =$

10. $\frac{1}{7} \div \frac{3}{14} =$

11. $\frac{9}{14} \div \frac{18}{21} =$

12. $\frac{12}{14} \div \frac{6}{7} =$

13. $\frac{8}{9} \div \frac{6}{9} =$

14. $\frac{6}{7} \div \frac{2}{9} =$

15. $\frac{4}{5} \div \frac{16}{20} =$

16. $\frac{1}{6} \div \frac{5}{12} =$

17. $\frac{1}{5} \div \frac{3}{5} =$

18. $\frac{14}{15} \div \frac{14}{15} =$

19. $\frac{3}{7} \div \frac{9}{10} =$

20. $\frac{14}{16} \div \frac{15}{20} =$

Division of Fractions

EXAMPLE Invert the divisor. Multiply and simplify if necessary.

$$\frac{3}{5} \div \frac{2}{5} = \frac{3}{5} \times \frac{5}{2}$$

$$= \frac{3}{5} \times \frac{5}{2}^{1}$$

$$= \frac{3 \times 1}{1 \times 2}$$

$$= \frac{3}{2} = 1\frac{1}{2}$$

Directions Divide these fractions. Simplify the answers to the lowest terms.

1. $\frac{3}{7} \div \frac{1}{7} =$ _____

2. $\frac{6}{7} \div \frac{2}{9} =$ _____

3. $\frac{5}{13} \div \frac{25}{26} =$ _____

4. $\frac{15}{16} \div \frac{3}{8} =$ _____

5. $\frac{6}{13} \div \frac{2}{13} =$ _____

6. $\frac{3}{10} \div 1\frac{4}{5} =$ _____

7. $\frac{6}{11} \div 2\frac{1}{5} =$ _____

8. $\frac{4}{5} \div \frac{24}{25} =$ _____

9. $\frac{5}{7} \div \frac{14}{15} =$ _____

10. $\frac{1}{2} \div \frac{1}{3} =$ _____

11. $\frac{5}{2} \div 1\frac{1}{2} =$ _____

12. $\frac{4}{3} \div 2\frac{1}{5} =$ _____

13. $\frac{1}{5} \div \frac{3}{4} =$ _____

14. $\frac{9}{10} \div \frac{2}{5} =$ _____

15. $\frac{2}{5} \div \frac{1}{8} =$ _____

16. $5\frac{2}{8} \div \frac{1}{8} =$ _____

17. $\frac{12}{17} \div \frac{15}{21} =$ _____

18. $\frac{1}{3} \div 2\frac{1}{2} =$ _____

19. $2\frac{3}{4} \div \frac{11}{16} =$ _____

20. $5\frac{3}{5} \div 2\frac{1}{10} =$ _____

21. $2\frac{1}{5} \div \frac{1}{5} =$ _____

22. $3\frac{2}{7} \div \frac{46}{21} =$ _____

23. $1\frac{2}{5} \div 2\frac{2}{3} =$ _____

24. $1\frac{2}{8} \div 2\frac{1}{2} =$ _____

25. $\frac{5}{16} \div 1\frac{1}{2} =$ _____

26. $7\frac{1}{2} \div 22\frac{1}{2} =$ _____

27. $5\frac{2}{3} \div 1\frac{5}{12} =$ _____

28. $\frac{3}{7} \div 1\frac{3}{11} =$ _____

29. $2\frac{1}{6} \div 1\frac{1}{2} =$ _____

30. $3\frac{5}{13} \div \frac{22}{39} =$ _____

31. $5 \div 1\frac{1}{6} =$ _____

32. $11 \div 3\frac{4}{33} =$ _____

33. $4\frac{3}{11} \div 6 =$ _____

34. $4\frac{1}{2} \div \frac{36}{38} =$ _____

35. $3\frac{2}{7} \div 1\frac{1}{2} =$ _____

36. $2\frac{5}{6} \div 17 =$ _____

37. $1\frac{5}{9} \div 1\frac{2}{5} =$ _____

38. $2\frac{3}{5} \div \frac{1}{5} =$ _____

39. $5\frac{3}{8} \div 1\frac{1}{16} =$ _____

40. $1\frac{3}{11} \div 5 =$ _____

More Addition of Fractions

EXAMPLE   To add fractions and mixed numbers with unlike denominators, find the least common multiple of the denominators. Raise the fraction to higher terms and add.

$$\frac{5}{9} = \frac{35}{63}$$
$$+ \frac{3}{7} = + \frac{27}{63}$$
$$= \frac{62}{63}$$

Directions Add these fractions. Simplify the answers.

1. $\frac{11}{20}$ $+ \frac{4}{7}$

2. $\frac{5}{11}$ $+ \frac{4}{7}$

3. $2\frac{5}{7}$ $+ 5\frac{6}{8}$

4. $5\frac{4}{9}$ $+ 3\frac{2}{11}$

5. $16\frac{5}{12}$ $+ 4\frac{3}{5}$

6. $\frac{3}{13}$ $+ \frac{1}{5}$

7. $\frac{3}{7}$ $+ \frac{9}{9}$

8. $\frac{5}{12}$ $+ 6\frac{4}{10}$

9. $6\frac{3}{13}$ $+ 4\frac{5}{6}$

10. $9\frac{5}{11}$ $+ 6\frac{2}{5}$

11. $\frac{6}{22}$ $+ \frac{4}{5}$

12. $\frac{7}{11}$ $+ \frac{10}{12}$

13. $2\frac{7}{13}$ $+ 9\frac{3}{10}$

14. $3\frac{5}{7}$ $+ 2\frac{9}{11}$

15. $4\frac{7}{13}$ $+ 2\frac{3}{5}$

16. $3\frac{4}{7}$ $+ 7\frac{3}{8}$

17. $28\frac{5}{7}$ $+ 6\frac{4}{9}$

18. $4\frac{1}{12}$ $+ 6\frac{2}{7}$

19. $35\frac{4}{19}$ $+ 2\frac{3}{10}$

20. $12\frac{8}{15}$ $+ \frac{1}{4}$

Addition of Mixed Numbers

EXAMPLE Add the fractions. Find the lowest common multiple if necessary.
Add the whole numbers. Simplify to lowest terms.

$$3\frac{2}{13}$$
$$+\ 4\frac{1}{13}$$
$$\overline{\quad 7\frac{3}{13}}$$

Directions Add these fractions. Simplify the answers to the lowest terms.

1. $2\frac{3}{10}$
$+\ 3\frac{1}{10}$
_____

2. $18\frac{5}{16}$
$+\ 3\frac{1}{8}$
_____

3. $81\frac{2}{15}$
$+\ 2\frac{2}{3}$
_____

4. $18\frac{2}{11}$
$+\ 4\frac{5}{6}$
_____

5. $23\frac{4}{7}$
$+\ 8$
_____

6. $4\frac{2}{5}$
$+\ 3\frac{1}{5}$
_____

7. $7\frac{1}{4}$
$+\ \frac{1}{3}$
_____

8. 17
$+\ 2\frac{1}{5}$
_____

9. $29\frac{2}{5}$
$+\ 3\frac{5}{6}$
_____

10. $16\frac{3}{13}$
$+\ \frac{4}{39}$
_____

11. $6\frac{5}{21}$
$+\ 2\frac{1}{7}$
_____

12. $13\frac{5}{16}$
$+\ 2\frac{1}{4}$
_____

13. $10\frac{3}{7}$
$+\ 2\frac{4}{5}$
_____

14. $13\frac{3}{22}$
$+\ 5\frac{3}{44}$
_____

Directions Rewrite the fractions in the standard form and add.
Simplify the answers to the lowest terms.

15. $1\frac{1}{2} + 2\frac{3}{11} =$ _____

16. $2\frac{3}{5} + 4\frac{1}{6} =$ _____

17. $7\frac{1}{7} + 5\frac{1}{8} =$ _____

18. $6\frac{2}{9} + 1\frac{3}{10} =$ _____

19. $10 + 2\frac{1}{6} =$ _____

20. $5\frac{2}{12} + \frac{1}{10} =$ _____

Subtraction of Fractions with Like Denominators

EXAMPLE   Subtract numerators. Keep denominators.
Simplify if necessary.

$$\frac{7}{8} - \frac{3}{8} = \frac{4}{8} = \frac{1}{2}$$

Directions Subtract these fractions and simplify your answers.

1. $\frac{18}{35} - \frac{9}{35}$

2. $3\frac{7}{12} - 2\frac{2}{12}$

3. $8\frac{13}{15} - 3\frac{4}{15}$

4. $16\frac{11}{20} - \frac{6}{20}$

5. $7\frac{2}{33} - 5$

6. $\frac{13}{16} - \frac{5}{16}$

7. $5\frac{15}{18} - 2\frac{3}{18}$

8. $11\frac{12}{41} - 5\frac{6}{41}$

9. $8\frac{5}{28} - 5$

10. $13\frac{17}{18} - 4\frac{8}{18}$

11. $\frac{10}{21} - \frac{7}{21}$

12. $11\frac{4}{10} - \frac{1}{10}$

13. $30\frac{18}{33} - 5\frac{7}{33}$

14. $31\frac{14}{27} - 4\frac{5}{27}$

15. $15\frac{3}{16} - 4\frac{1}{16}$

16. $13\frac{4}{29} - 3\frac{2}{29}$

17. $8\frac{33}{56} - 2\frac{5}{56}$

18. $33\frac{37}{45} - \frac{2}{45}$

19. $13\frac{17}{38} - \frac{7}{38}$

20. $25\frac{7}{33} - 4\frac{4}{33}$

Subtraction of Fractions Without Renaming

EXAMPLE   Raise fractions to higher terms. Subtract numerators and whole numbers. Simplify if necessary.

$$
\begin{array}{rcl}
15\frac{2}{3} &=& 15\frac{14}{21} \\
-\ 6\frac{2}{7} &=& -\ 6\frac{6}{21} \\
\hline
&=& 9\frac{8}{21}
\end{array}
$$

Directions   Subtract these fractions. Simplify the answers to the lowest terms.

1. $25\frac{1}{8}$
  $-\ 24\frac{1}{9}$

2. $28\frac{12}{15}$
  $-\ 4\frac{2}{5}$

3. $52\frac{3}{10}$
  $-\ 2\frac{5}{17}$

4. $3\frac{15}{21}$
  $-\ 1\frac{1}{5}$

5. $51\frac{5}{9}$
  $-\ 4\frac{4}{10}$

6. $22\frac{7}{8}$
  $-\ 3\frac{1}{24}$

7. $26\frac{4}{9}$
  $-\ 4\frac{1}{8}$

8. $14\frac{5}{11}$
  $-\ 7\frac{2}{7}$

9. $7\frac{2}{18}$
  $-\ 5\frac{1}{20}$

10. $28\frac{4}{21}$
  $-\ 4\frac{1}{7}$

11. $25\frac{12}{38}$
  $-\ 9\frac{3}{19}$

12. $33\frac{4}{7}$
  $-\ 6\frac{1}{7}$

13. $4\frac{11}{16}$
  $-\ 2\frac{3}{32}$

14. $16\frac{7}{28}$
  $-\ 5\frac{3}{28}$

15. $16\frac{3}{10}$
  $-\ 2\frac{1}{5}$

16. $8\frac{1}{2}$
  $-\ 5\frac{3}{9}$

17. $42\frac{6}{7}$
  $-\ 5\frac{1}{6}$

18. $2\frac{1}{3}$
  $-\ 1\frac{2}{15}$

19. $5\frac{1}{13}$
  $-\ 2\frac{1}{15}$

20. $14\frac{2}{15}$
  $-\ \frac{1}{16}$

Subtraction of Fractions with Renaming

EXAMPLE   Rename the fractions and subtract them. Subtract the whole numbers.
Simplify if necessary.

$$19\frac{1}{5} = 18\frac{6}{5}$$
$$-\ 2\frac{3}{5} = -\ 2\frac{3}{5}$$
$$\overline{16\frac{3}{5}}$$

Directions Subtract these fractions. Simplify the answers to the lowest terms.

1. $13\frac{1}{8}$
$-\ 1\frac{7}{8}$

2. $28\frac{1}{3}$
$-\ 5\frac{2}{3}$

3. $13\frac{2}{19}$
$-\ 2\frac{5}{19}$

4. $14\frac{2}{17}$
$-\ 5\frac{3}{17}$

5. $26\frac{5}{28}$
$-\ 4\frac{6}{28}$

6. $28\frac{2}{7}$
$-\ 5\frac{5}{7}$

7. $4\frac{3}{9}$
$-\ \frac{5}{9}$

8. $6\frac{4}{11}$
$-\ 1\frac{6}{11}$

9. $29\frac{5}{17}$
$-\ 28\frac{9}{17}$

10. $42\frac{16}{50}$
$-\ 2\frac{25}{50}$

11. $12\frac{2}{17}$
$-\ 3\frac{5}{17}$

12. 6
$-\ \frac{3}{12}$

13. $8\frac{3}{21}$
$-\ 5\frac{7}{21}$

14. $32\frac{13}{35}$
$-\ 5\frac{15}{35}$

15. 32
$-\ 4\frac{5}{22}$

16. 7
$-\ 5\frac{11}{12}$

17. 67
$-\ 5\frac{17}{18}$

18. $8\frac{7}{20}$
$-\ 5\frac{11}{20}$

19. 5
$-\ 2\frac{17}{20}$

20. $9\frac{11}{20}$
$-\ 5\frac{12}{20}$

More Subtraction of Fractions with Renaming

EXAMPLE   Rename the fractions and subtract them. Subtract the whole numbers.
Simplify if necessary.

$$3\frac{2}{5} \quad = \quad 3\frac{16}{40} \quad = \quad 2\frac{56}{40}$$
$$-\;2\frac{7}{8} \quad = \quad -\;2\frac{35}{40} \quad = \quad -\;2\frac{35}{40}$$
$$\overline{\qquad\qquad\qquad\qquad\qquad\qquad\quad \frac{21}{40}}$$

Directions   Subtract these fractions. Simplify the answers.

1. $4\frac{3}{4}$
   $-\;3\frac{5}{6}$

2. $14\frac{2}{9}$
   $-\;5\frac{7}{8}$

3. $11\frac{1}{5}$
   $-\;\frac{1}{4}$

4. $38\frac{2}{11}$
   $-\;4\frac{5}{22}$

5. $45\frac{9}{11}$
   $-\;4\frac{21}{22}$

6. $6\frac{4}{13}$
   $-\;5\frac{25}{26}$

7. $16\frac{9}{13}$
   $-\;4\frac{18}{26}$

8. $29\frac{1}{15}$
   $-\;2\frac{3}{4}$

9. 12
   $-\;2\frac{10}{11}$

10. $11\frac{1}{16}$
   $-\;\frac{1}{2}$

11. 4
   $-\;2\frac{3}{5}$

12. $3\frac{1}{2}$
   $-\;2\frac{6}{7}$

13. $18\frac{2}{15}$
   $-\;5\frac{3}{4}$

14. $13\frac{3}{16}$
   $-\;4\frac{7}{8}$

15. $23\frac{4}{7}$
   $-\;22\frac{9}{14}$

16. $9\frac{1}{3}$
   $-\;4\frac{11}{13}$

17. $12\frac{14}{15}$
   $-\;10\frac{29}{30}$

18. $10\frac{2}{5}$
   $-\;5\frac{10}{11}$

19. $10\frac{2}{7}$
   $-\;8\frac{11}{14}$

20. $4\frac{5}{16}$
   $-\;2\frac{3}{8}$

Subtraction of Fractions

EXAMPLE   Change to common denominators if necessary. Rename top
mixed number if necessary. Subtract numerators. Simplify if necessary.

$$1\frac{7}{18} = 1\frac{7}{18} = \frac{25}{18}$$
$$-\frac{5}{9} = -\frac{10}{18} = -\frac{10}{18}$$
$$\frac{15}{18} = \frac{5}{6}$$

Directions Subtract these fractions. Simplify the answers to the lowest terms.

1. $\frac{7}{18}$
$-\frac{3}{18}$

5. $2\frac{5}{13}$
$-\frac{4}{13}$

9. $16\frac{2}{7}$
$-2\frac{3}{7}$

13. $16\frac{3}{10}$
$-1\frac{5}{10}$

2. $16\frac{12}{13}$
$-3\frac{1}{26}$

6. $4\frac{15}{16}$
$-2\frac{3}{8}$

10. $10\frac{13}{24}$
$-2\frac{1}{6}$

14. $7\frac{5}{11}$
-3

3. $33\frac{1}{5}$
$-2\frac{3}{4}$

7. 18
$-5\frac{2}{7}$

11. 13
$-2\frac{3}{11}$

15. $59\frac{1}{15}$
$-2\frac{3}{45}$

4. $23\frac{7}{18}$
$-\frac{3}{72}$

8. $5\frac{1}{10}$
$-2\frac{7}{15}$

12. 12
$-6\frac{3}{13}$

16. $12\frac{3}{16}$
$-5\frac{11}{48}$

Directions Rewrite the fractions in the standard form and subtract.
Simplify the answers to the lowest terms.

17. $3\frac{1}{4} - 2\frac{7}{8} =$ _____

19. $6\frac{5}{12} - 4\frac{1}{5} =$ _____

18. $13\frac{2}{15} - 3\frac{4}{5} =$ _____

20. $38 - 2\frac{3}{7} =$ _____

Basic Operations with Fractions and Mixed Numbers

	Add.	Subtract.	Multiply.	Divide.

EXAMPLES

Add.

$$\frac{3}{4}$$
$$+ \frac{3}{4}$$
$$\overline{\frac{6}{4}} = 1\frac{1}{2}$$

Subtract.

$$1\frac{5}{8}$$
$$- 1\frac{3}{8}$$
$$\overline{\frac{2}{8}} = \frac{1}{4}$$

Multiply.

$$\overset{1}{\underset{1}{\cancel{\frac{2}{3}}}} \times \overset{1}{\underset{5}{\cancel{\frac{3}{10}}}} = \frac{1}{5}$$

Divide.

$$\frac{1}{4} \div \frac{7}{8} = \frac{1}{\underset{1}{\cancel{4}}} \times \overset{2}{\cancel{\frac{8}{7}}} = \frac{2}{7}$$

Directions Add.

1. $2\frac{1}{3} + 3\frac{1}{3} =$ _____

2. $4\frac{1}{8} + 2\frac{2}{8} =$ _____

3. $1\frac{1}{5} + \frac{1}{10} =$ _____

4. $2\frac{1}{6} + 3\frac{2}{3} =$ _____

5. $4\frac{1}{7} + 1\frac{3}{14} =$ _____

6. $1\frac{1}{8} + 2\frac{1}{6} =$ _____

Directions Subtract.

7. $5\frac{2}{8} - 1\frac{1}{4} =$ _____

8. $2\frac{2}{3} - 1\frac{1}{2} =$ _____

9. $4\frac{7}{8} - 1\frac{3}{4} =$ _____

10. $6\frac{2}{8} - 2\frac{3}{4} =$ _____

11. $35 - 6\frac{2}{7} =$ _____

12. $41\frac{3}{5} - 6 =$ _____

Directions Multiply.

13. $\frac{5}{6} \times \frac{2}{3} =$ _____

14. $\frac{4}{11} \times \frac{22}{10} =$ _____

15. $\frac{1}{2} \times \frac{2}{3} =$ _____

16. $2\frac{3}{5} \times 1\frac{1}{3} =$ _____

17. $6\frac{2}{9} \times \frac{1}{2} =$ _____

18. $1\frac{1}{8} \times 2\frac{3}{5} =$ _____

Directions Divide.

19. $\frac{6}{8} \div \frac{18}{24} =$ _____

20. $\frac{5}{6} \div \frac{25}{30} =$ _____

21. $\frac{4}{11} \div \frac{18}{20} =$ _____

22. $1\frac{1}{2} \div \frac{3}{6} =$ _____

23. $2\frac{1}{4} \div \frac{9}{10} =$ _____

24. $2\frac{3}{5} \div \frac{26}{30} =$ _____

25. $1\frac{2}{9} \div 1\frac{1}{2} =$ _____

Place Value

EXAMPLE　　Look at the underlined digit. Write the place value for the underlined digit.

3.7<u>5</u>4 _____hundredths_____

Directions Write the place value for each underlined digit.

1. 2.3<u>4</u> _____

2. 1.2<u>0</u>345 _____

3. 1.023<u>0</u>1 _____

4. 12.<u>0</u>1012 _____

5. 0.00<u>0</u>12 _____

6. 12.0020<u>0</u> _____

7. 1.2<u>2</u>008 _____

8. 840.<u>8</u>8940 _____

9. 2.1076<u>9</u> _____

10. 502.00<u>1</u> _____

11. 3.400<u>1</u> _____

12. 7.<u>3</u>309 _____

13. 1.0<u>0</u>23 _____

14. 0.002<u>0</u>03 _____

15. 3.0041<u>0</u> _____

16. 23.000<u>1</u>9 _____

Directions Underline the place value indicated.

17. 12.0002　　ten-thousandths

18. 0.012　　tenths

19. 0.00023　　hundred-thousandths

20. 0.00012　　thousandths

21. 1.02304　　tenths

22. 102.0023　　tenths

23. 3.04958　　ten-thousandths

24. 0.010102　　millionths

25. 2.09077　　hundred-thousandths

26. 10.10230　　hundred-thousandths

27. 530.0002　　tenths

28. 2.93001　　ten-thousandths

29. 0.0112887　　millionths

30. 1.0234　　tenths

Reading and Writing Numerals

EXAMPLES Look at the underlined digit. Write the name of the place.

3.14<u>3</u>   <u>thousandths</u>

Start at the left. Write the word for the numerals.
Use *and* to stand for the decimal point.

1.63   <u>one and sixty-three hundredths</u>

Directions Write the name of the place for each underlined digit.

1. 12.1<u>8</u> _____	**9.** 8.0<u>2</u>63 _____	**17.** 3.<u>0</u>4 _____
2. 0.9<u>2</u>0 _____	**10.** 4.000<u>5</u> _____	**18.** 0.003<u>7</u>05 _____
3. 1.03<u>4</u> _____	**11.** 4.59<u>2</u>1 _____	**19.** 0.003<u>0</u>4 _____
4. 3.05<u>7</u>8 _____	**12.** 295.1<u>1</u> _____	**20.** 59.0<u>4</u>92 _____
5. 64.23<u>8</u>1 _____	**13.** 5.02<u>8</u>48 _____	**21.** 83.3<u>9</u>051 _____
6. 0.0<u>0</u>3 _____	**14.** 45.9221<u>0</u> _____	**22.** 19.460<u>3</u>1 _____
7. 152.<u>9</u> _____	**15.** 394.0<u>2</u>64 _____	**23.** 44.<u>9</u>12 _____
8. 24.022<u>3</u>1 _____	**16.** 385.0448<u>5</u> _____	**24.** 5.6105<u>6</u> _____

Directions Write the following numerals in words.

25. 9.032 _____

_____

26. 0.0024 _____

_____

27. 102.10245 _____

_____

28. 0.010139 _____

_____

29. 40.044 _____

_____

30. 410.00003 _____

_____

Translation of Decimal Numbers

EXAMPLE   Read the amount. Write it in numerals. Remember, *and* stands for the decimal point.

Five and seventy-one hundredths   _____5.71_____

Directions   Write the following amounts in numerals.

1. Twenty-three and six tenths   _____

2. Forty-one and three hundredths   _____

3. Seventy-two thousandths   _____

4. Five and eight tenths   _____

5. Six and three thousandths   _____

6. One hundred two thousandths   _____

7. Four hundred three thousandths   _____

8. Two and two hundredths   _____

9. Six hundred thirty-four ten-thousandths   _____

10. Six thousand, three hundred forty-eight hundred-thousandths   _____

11. Twenty thousand, four hundred five hundred-thousandths   _____

12. One hundred two and seven hundredths   _____

13. Eight hundred two and seven hundred fifty-one thousandths   _____

14. One thousand, nine hundred three and seven hundredths   _____

15. Two thousand and twenty-six thousandths   _____

16. Four thousand three and seven ten-thousandths   _____

17. Two hundred six thousandths   _____

18. Three hundred-thousandths   _____

19. Thirty-four hundred-thousandths   _____

20. One and fifty-nine hundredths   _____

Comparing and Rounding Decimals

EXAMPLE Order numbers from least to greatest.

                       Least ——————→ Greatest

    1.059   0.0159   0.159   0.0159   0.159   1.059

Directions Arrange each set in order from least to greatest.

1. 0.6234   62.350   0.7406   _____ _____ _____

2. 0.0045   0.0450   0.0040   _____ _____ _____

3. 2.0049   2.0050   2.034   _____ _____ _____

4. 0.1024   0.1031   0.113   _____ _____ _____

5. 23.0045   23.004   2.30045   _____ _____ _____

6. 304.097   300.999   304.102   _____ _____ _____

7. 3.00495   30.0495   0.300495   _____ _____ _____

8. 9.00603   9.00599   9.000999   _____ _____ _____

9. 0.356924   0.350899   0.400001   _____ _____ _____

10. 5.04592   6.001   0.939401   _____ _____ _____

EXAMPLE Round to the nearest hundredth. Round up if thousandth is 5 or greater.
    5.136
    5.14

Directions Round the following numbers to the nearest:

Tenth	Hundredth	Thousandth
11. 245.44 _____	**19.** 0.0394 _____	**28.** 0.08931 _____
12. 4.091 _____	**20.** 199.051 _____	**29.** 0.00592 _____
13. 2.0399 _____	**21.** 6.34499 _____	**30.** 10.122309 _____
14. 0.048 _____	**22.** 0.995 _____	**31.** 0.39 _____
15. 30.9199 _____	**23.** 666.034 _____	**32.** 390.0485 _____
16. 0.048539 _____	**24.** 394.091999 _____	**33.** 3,998.0002 _____
17. 5.0555 _____	**25.** 0.0951 _____	**34.** 8.89099 _____
18. 49.952 _____	**26.** 495.0495 _____	**35.** 4.76842 _____
	27. 40.0495 _____	

Addition of Decimals

EXAMPLE   Write the problem in vertical form. Then add.

$$2.3 + 4 + 0.09 + 59 =$$

```
  2.3        2.30
  4.         4.00
  0.09       0.09
+ 59.      + 59.00
 65.39      65.39
```

Directions Rewrite the following addends in vertical form and add.

1. $3.4 + 5 + 0.18 + 17 =$ _____

2. $0.056 + 3.02 + 4 + 1.2 =$ _____

3. $19 + 9.3 + 0.049 + 3 =$ _____

4. $30.9 + 5 + 0.91 + 0.922 =$ _____

5. $0.08 + 1 + 1.1 + 6.2 =$ _____

6. $2.331 + 0.1123 + 7 + 1.8 =$ _____

7. $16 + 4.05 + 5 + 4.77 =$ _____

8. $65.94 + 4.7 + 1 + 7.2 =$ _____

9. $5.906 + 0.071 + 44.581 =$ _____

10. $3.045 + 0.045 + 84.3 =$ _____

11. $0.9639 + 0.0082 + 5.03 =$ _____

12. $7.304 + 1.5 + 8.33 + 2 =$ _____

13. $7004.1 + 35.066 + 0.06 =$ _____

14. $93 + 0.739 + 2.38 + 0.1 =$ _____

15. $4.4 + 3.5 + 23.49 + 6 =$ _____

16. $6.06 + 33 + 0.045 + 3 =$ _____

17. $5 + 6 + 6.9 + 0.082 =$ _____

18. $6.112 + 4.7 + 6 + 0.0001 =$ _____

19. $9.9 + 5.03 + 5.5 + 0.002 =$ _____

20. $47.05 + 6.2 + 0.4 + 1 =$ _____

21. $54 + 2.2 + 0.01 + 6.9 =$ _____

22. $2.334 + 0.1128 + 8.3 =$ _____

23. $4.056 + 3.5 + 7 + 0.92 =$ _____

24. $5 + 6.1 + 55.6 + 0.01 =$ _____

25. $6.001 + 4.9 + 3 + 0.05 =$ _____

26. $1 + 2.1 + 5.66 + 0.031 =$ _____

27. $9.9 + 3.4 + 0.56 + 0.012 =$ _____

28. $6.035 + 3.4 + 5 + 0.057 =$ _____

Directions Solve the following word problems with addition.

29. Compute the total amount deposited if Lance's deposits are $15, $1.90, $121, and $2.65. _____

30. It rains three times during the first week of summer vacation. Compute the total amount if it rains 2.05 inches, 0.29 inches, and 3 inches. _____

Subtraction of Decimals

EXAMPLE Write the problem in vertical form. Then subtract.

$1.03 - 0.94 =$

```
   0 9 13
   1.03
 - 0.94
   0.09
```

Directions Rewrite these problems in vertical form. Then subtract.

1. 6.34 − 0.14 = _____

2. From 23.034 subtract 0.0341 _____

3. 20 − 0.934 = _____

4. Subtract 12.92 from 27.104 _____

5. 103.506 − 94 = _____

6. Subtract 0.607 from 2 _____

7. 2.3941 − 0.2852 = _____

8. From 1.0182 subtract 0.81818 _____

9. 34.8 − 5.0837 = _____

10. From 2 subtract 1.9283 _____

11. 0.0238 − 0.003856 = _____

12. Subtract 9.9 from 10.005 _____

13. 1.3 − 1.0953 = _____

14. Subtract 0.0056 from 0.9 _____

15. 58.3 − 12.923 = _____

16. From 4.95 subtract 2.5 _____

17. 71 − 5.341 = _____

18. Subtract 0.3945 from 6 _____

19. 0.304 − 0.0433 = _____

20. From 205.5 subtract 0.56 _____

21. 4.59 − 2.4 = _____

22. Subtract 2.3 from 5 _____

23. 4.5 − 0.0954 = _____

24. From 6.94 subtract 0.9567 _____

25. 49 − 5.607 = _____

26. Subtract 0.0384 from 1.991 _____

27. 3 − 0.4581 = _____

28. From 86 subtract 0.86 _____

Directions Solve the following word problems with subtraction.

29. Diana saves $25 for school clothes and purchases a blouse costing $9.96. How much money does she have left? _____

30. Ross drives 298.6 miles on a two-day vacation. If he drives 150 miles on the first day, how many miles does he drive on the second day? _____

Multiplication of Decimals by Powers of Ten

(EXAMPLE) Write the problem in vertical form.
Then multiply. Remember the decimal point.
$2.63 \times 10 =$

$$\begin{array}{r} 2.63 \\ \times\ 10 \\ \hline 26.30 \end{array}$$

Directions Rewrite the following problems in vertical form and multiply.

1. $6.25 \times 10 =$ _____

2. $5.638 \times 10 =$ _____

3. $0.06 \times 100 =$ _____

4. $0.072 \times 100 =$ _____

5. $1.061 \times 10 =$ _____

6. $5.63 \times 100 =$ _____

7. $3.14 \times 100 =$ _____

8. $1.414 \times 1,000 =$ _____

9. $0.00627 \times 1,000 =$ _____

10. $0.2802 \times 10 =$ _____

11. $0.0605 \times 100 =$ _____

12. $0.7701 \times 100 =$ _____

13. $1.101 \times 1,000 =$ _____

14. $7.6 \times 100 =$ _____

15. $5.1 \times 1,000 =$ _____

16. $8.81 \times 10,000 =$ _____

17. $3.7 \times 10,000 =$ _____

18. $2.05 \times 10,000 =$ _____

19. $0.0001 \times 1,000 =$ _____

20. $5.6 \times 100 =$ _____

21. $69.1 \times 1,000 =$ _____

22. $0.777 \times 1,000 =$ _____

23. $0.201 \times 10,000 =$ _____

24. $0.028 \times 10 =$ _____

25. $0.002 \times 1,000 =$ _____

26. $1.1 \times 1,000 =$ _____

27. $10 \times 1.67 =$ _____

28. $1,000 \times 0.003 =$ _____

29. $100 \times 0.1505 =$ _____

30. $10 \times 1.688 =$ _____

31. $1,000 \times 3.9 =$ _____

32. $100 \times 3.702 =$ _____

33. $10 \times 0.1 =$ _____

34. $1,000 \times 0.11 =$ _____

35. $3.44 \times 100 =$ _____

36. $1.112 \times 1,000 =$ _____

37. $0.00232 \times 10,000 =$ _____

38. $0.012 \times 10,000 =$ _____

39. $3.033 \times 10 =$ _____

40. $8.014 \times 1,000 =$ _____

41. $0.0556 \times 10,000 =$ _____

42. $5.5 \times 100 =$ _____

43. $0.6709 \times 100 =$ _____

44. $0.0021 \times 1,000 =$ _____

45. $23.1 \times 100 =$ _____

Multiplication of Decimals

EXAMPLE   Write the problem in vertical form.
Then multiply. Remember the decimal point.
$1.2 \times 0.04 =$

$$\begin{array}{r} 1.2 \\ \times .04 \\ \hline 48 \\ 00 \\ \hline 0.048 \end{array}$$

Directions Rewrite the following problems in vertical form and multiply.

1. $3.5 \times 0.11 =$ _____

2. $48 \times 1.5 =$ _____

3. $4.05 \times 0.03 =$ _____

4. $3.6 \times 0.93 =$ _____

5. $56.7 \times 0.31 =$ _____

6. $0.059 \times 0.12 =$ _____

7. $9.01 \times 1.03 =$ _____

8. $5.8 \times 0.0004 =$ _____

9. $0.0034 \times 23 =$ _____

10. $6.12 \times 3.4 =$ _____

11. $7.81 \times 56 =$ _____

12. $5.25 \times 0.01 =$ _____

13. $6.79 \times 8.3 =$ _____

14. $0.044 \times 0.9 =$ _____

15. $0.09 \times 0.04 =$ _____

16. $7.05 \times 0.3 =$ _____

17. $98 \times 0.11 =$ _____

18. $0.931 \times 100 =$ _____

19. $7.02 \times 5.1 =$ _____

20. $0.034 \times 0.0048 =$ _____

21. $1,000 \times 0.00342 =$ _____

22. $405 \times 1.52 =$ _____

23. $8.8 \times 6.7 =$ _____

24. $13.5 \times 4.7 =$ _____

25. $69.1 \times 0.001 =$ _____

26. $10.4 \times 10.5 =$ _____

27. $0.059 \times 0.0691 =$ _____

28. $0.101 \times 121.1 =$ _____

Directions Solve the following word problems with multiplication.

29. Lionel works part-time with a construction company and earns $24.50 per day. How much will Lionel earn working 5 days? _____

30. Regina earns $7.50 per hour straight time. Compute Regina's time and one-half rate by finding the product of $7.50 and 1.5. _____

Scientific Notation with Positive Exponents

EXAMPLE   Write in scientific notation. $2,300,000 = 2.3 \times 10^6$ ←— an exponent

↑ a number between one and ten

↗ a power of ten

Directions Rewrite the following numbers using scientific notation.

1. $4,200 =$ _____

2. $6,250 =$ _____

3. $82,100 =$ _____

4. $50,000 =$ _____

5. $72,300 =$ _____

6. $15,080 =$ _____

7. $1,800 =$ _____

8. $29,000 =$ _____

9. $500,000 =$ _____

10. $600,000 =$ _____

11. $700,000,000 =$ _____

12. $7,800,000 =$ _____

13. $10,000 =$ _____

14. $35,600 =$ _____

15. $81.52 =$ _____

16. $17.63 =$ _____

17. $236.5 =$ _____

18. $3,800 =$ _____

19. $19,000 =$ _____

20. $16.12 =$ _____

21. $610,000,000 =$ _____

22. $400,000,000 =$ _____

23. $790,000 =$ _____

24. $25.33 =$ _____

25. $1,420,000 =$ _____

26. $1,000,000,000 =$ _____

27. $34,000,000 =$ _____

28. $103,000 =$ _____

29. $23,000 =$ _____

30. $450,000,000 =$ _____

31. $11,000 =$ _____

32. $401,300 =$ _____

33. $311,400 =$ _____

34. $102.3 =$ _____

35. $927,000 =$ _____

36. $211,400 =$ _____

37. $100,000 =$ _____

38. $10,000 =$ _____

39. $344,000,000,000 =$ _____

40. $42,000,000,000 =$ _____

41. $12,000,000 =$ _____

42. $41,000,000 =$ _____

43. $764,200,000 =$ _____

44. $911,400,000 =$ _____

45. $102,000 =$ _____

Scientific Notation with Negative Exponents

EXAMPLE Write in scientific notation. $0.006 = 6 \times 10^{-3}$ ◄— a negative exponent

↑ a number between one and ten

↗ a power of ten

Directions Rewrite the following numbers using scientific notation.

1. $0.008 =$ _____

2. $0.0715 =$ _____

3. $0.0062 =$ _____

4. $0.0007 =$ _____

5. $0.02 =$ _____

6. $0.0321 =$ _____

7. $0.0805 =$ _____

8. $0.0006 =$ _____

9. $0.00005 =$ _____

10. $0.03051 =$ _____

11. $0.00091 =$ _____

12. $0.0000007 =$ _____

13. $0.000003 =$ _____

14. $0.00000021 =$ _____

15. $0.0061 =$ _____

16. $0.00054 =$ _____

17. $0.000003 =$ _____

18. $0.00101 =$ _____

19. $0.000005 =$ _____

20. $0.000052 =$ _____

21. $0.000735 =$ _____

22. $0.0001433 =$ _____

23. $0.00021 =$ _____

24. $0.00093 =$ _____

25. $0.000000004 =$ _____

26. $0.00000000062 =$ _____

27. $0.423 =$ _____

28. $0.00316 =$ _____

29. $0.005071 =$ _____

30. $0.000078 =$ _____

31. $0.002103 =$ _____

32. $0.0000000005 =$ _____

33. $0.00000123 =$ _____

34. $0.00203 =$ _____

35. $0.000222 =$ _____

36. $0.0121 =$ _____

37. $0.10203 =$ _____

38. $0.000204 =$ _____

39. $0.0691 =$ _____

40. $0.0000203 =$ _____

41. $0.0000000304 =$ _____

42. $0.3044 =$ _____

43. $0.00077 =$ _____

44. $0.002058 =$ _____

45. $0.0004058 =$ _____

Scientific Notation in Standard Form

Write in standard form. 5.1×10^2 5.1×10^{-2}

$5\,.\,1\,0\,.\, = 510$ $0\,.\,0\,5\,.\,1 = 0.051$
     1 2   2 1

Directions Rewrite each scientific notation in standard form.

1. $5.6 \times 10^2 =$ _____

2. $1.5 \times 10^2 =$ _____

3. $2 \times 10^4 =$ _____

4. $8 \times 10^3 =$ _____

5. $4.65 \times 10^3 =$ _____

6. $1.73 \times 10^4 =$ _____

7. $6.203 \times 10^5 =$ _____

8. $2.414 \times 10^5 =$ _____

9. $8.5 \times 10^7 =$ _____

10. $3 \times 10^7 =$ _____

11. $2 \times 10^1 =$ _____

12. $5.16 \times 10^2 =$ _____

13. $8.2 \times 10^3 =$ _____

14. $1.2 \times 10^1 =$ _____

15. $7.502 \times 10^2 =$ _____

16. $3.0052 \times 10^2 =$ _____

17. $2.61 \times 10^3 =$ _____

18. $5.85 \times 10^4 =$ _____

19. $7.05 \times 10^4 =$ _____

20. $6 \times 10^4 =$ _____

21. $3.008 \times 10^3 =$ _____

22. $1.9 \times 10^2 =$ _____

23. $4.002 \times 10^4 =$ _____

24. $7 \times 10^{10} =$ _____

25. $1.9 \times 10^{-8} =$ _____

26. $3 \times 10^{-9} =$ _____

27. $5.03 \times 10^{-1} =$ _____

28. $4.06 \times 10^{-4} =$ _____

29. $6.003 \times 10^{-5} =$ _____

30. $1.01 \times 10^{-5} =$ _____

31. $4.5 \times 10^{-5} =$ _____

32. $5.012 \times 10^{-3} =$ _____

33. $6 \times 10^{-5} =$ _____

34. $7.01 \times 10^{-4} =$ _____

35. $2.34 \times 10^{-3} =$ _____

36. $4.535 \times 10^{-2} =$ _____

37. $1 \times 10^{-8} =$ _____

38. $1.024 \times 10^{-2} =$ _____

39. $4.441 \times 10^{-5} =$ _____

40. $7.002 \times 10^{-4} =$ _____

41. $2.001 \times 10^{-8} =$ _____

42. $3.3 \times 10^{-3} =$ _____

43. $6.77 \times 10^{-4} =$ _____

44. $4.001 \times 10^{-3} =$ _____

45. $5 \times 10^{-10} =$ _____

Scientific Notation

EXAMPLE   Write in scientific notation. $0.00563 = 0.005.63 = 5.63 \times 10^{-3}$
                                                                1 2 3

Directions Rewrite the following numbers using scientific notation.

1. $2,300,000 =$ _____

2. $59,000 =$ _____

3. $0.0005 =$ _____

4. $0.0000039 =$ _____

5. $23.41 =$ _____

6. $453 =$ _____

7. $25,400,000 =$ _____

8. $0.000000000843 =$ _____

9. $1,900,000,000 =$ _____

10. $39,400,000 =$ _____

11. $0.00000837 =$ _____

12. $567.2 =$ _____

13. $0.0001 =$ _____

14. $4,000 =$ _____

15. $0.00495 =$ _____

16. $567,000,000,000,000 =$ _____

EXAMPLE   Write in standard form. $5.63 \times 10^{-3} = 0.005.63 = 0.00563$
                                                             3 2 1

Directions Write the following numbers in standard form without exponents.

17. $2.3 \times 10^3 =$ _____

18. $4.29 \times 10^5 =$ _____

19. $8 \times 10^6 =$ _____

20. $5.7 \times 10^5 =$ _____

21. $4.94 \times 10^{-8} =$ _____

22. $7.03 \times 10^{-7} =$ _____

23. $6.1 \times 10^{10} =$ _____

24. $5.5 \times 10^{-3} =$ _____

25. $6.832 \times 10^6 =$ _____

26. $8.11 \times 10^{-2} =$ _____

27. $3 \times 10^{12} =$ _____

28. $1.35 \times 10^{-5} =$ _____

29. $1.39 \times 10^7 =$ _____

30. $9.04 \times 10^{-4} =$ _____

Division of Decimals by Powers of Ten

EXAMPLE   Write in standard form. Divide $53 \div 10 =$

$$
\begin{array}{r}
5.3 \\
10\overline{)53.0} \\
-\ 50 \\
\hline
3\ 0 \\
-\ 3\ 0 \\
\hline
0
\end{array}
$$

Directions   Rewrite the following division problems in the standard form and divide.

1. $62 \div 10 =$ _____

2. $7.7 \div 100 =$ _____

3. $0.07 \div 100 =$ _____

4. $39 \div 1,000 =$ _____

5. $3 \div 10 =$ _____

6. $4.07 \div 100 =$ _____

7. $3.02 \div 100 =$ _____

8. $8.4 \div 1,000 =$ _____

9. $100 \div 1,000 =$ _____

10. $5.6 \div 10 =$ _____

11. $7 \div 100 =$ _____

12. $6.2 \div 1,000 =$ _____

13. $1.8 \div 1,000 =$ _____

14. $94 \div 100 =$ _____

15. $5 \div 1,000 =$ _____

16. $13 \div 1,000 =$ _____

17. $2.6 \div 1,000 =$ _____

18. $8.6 \div 100 =$ _____

19. $0.0023 \div 10 =$ _____

20. $2 \div 1,000 =$ _____

21. $3.8 \div 100 =$ _____

22. $4.02 \div 10,000 =$ _____

23. $566 \div 1,000 =$ _____

24. $2,963 \div 1,000 =$ _____

25. $8,203 \div 10,000 =$ _____

26. $4,002 \div 100 =$ _____

27. $0.706 \div 10 =$ _____

28. $9 \div 1,000 =$ _____

29. $0.04 \div 100 =$ _____

30. $0.3006 \div 100 =$ _____

31. $0.35 \div 1,000 =$ _____

32. $4.02 \div 100 =$ _____

33. $17 \div 1,000 =$ _____

34. $1 \div 1,000 =$ _____

35. $4.2 \div 10,000 =$ _____

36. $0.02 \div 10,000 =$ _____

37. $45.7 \div 10,000 =$ _____

38. $5,023.5 \div 10,000 =$ _____

39. $51.5 \div 1,000 =$ _____

40. $6.66 \div 10,000 =$ _____

41. $3.02 \div 1,000 =$ _____

42. $728 \div 10 =$ _____

43. $936 \div 10,000 =$ _____

44. $641.02 \div 10,000 =$ _____

45. $5.5 \div 100 =$ _____

Division of Decimals

EXAMPLE

Write in standard form.
Move decimal. Divide 23.4 by 0.1 =

$$
\begin{array}{r}
234 \\
0.1\overline{)23.4} \\
-2 \\
\hline
03 \\
-3 \\
\hline
04 \\
-4 \\
\hline
0
\end{array}
$$

Directions Rewrite the following division problems in the standard form
and divide. Round each quotient to the nearest hundredth.

1. $14.4 \div 0.7 =$ _____

2. $0.46 \div 0.4 =$ _____

3. $0.98 \div 0.8 =$ _____

4. $10 \div 5.5 =$ _____

5. $1.5 \div 0.9 =$ _____

6. $2.6 \div 1.5 =$ _____

7. $0.06 \div 0.7 =$ _____

8. $40 \div 1.2 =$ _____

9. $7.7 \div 0.03 =$ _____

10. $5.6 \div 0.12 =$ _____

11. $12.3 \div 1.1 =$ _____

12. $6.99 \div 1.2 =$ _____

13. $9.12 \div 0.9 =$ _____

14. $28.04 \div 0.7 =$ _____

15. $3.5 \div 3 =$ _____

16. $6.33 \div 0.07 =$ _____

17. $1 \div 0.9 =$ _____

18. $2.2 \div 13 =$ _____

19. $30 \div 89 =$ _____

20. $5.06 \div 1.2 =$ _____

21. $5 \div 1.5 =$ _____

22. $49.9 \div 3.4 =$ _____

23. $2 \div 4.5 =$ _____

24. $0.506 \div 0.403 =$ _____

25. $4.06 \div 2.02 =$ _____

26. $0.0008 \div 0.04 =$ _____

27. $0.045 \div 0.08 =$ _____

28. $3.91 \div 2.6 =$ _____

Directions Solve the following word problems with division.

29. Kathleen purchases tomatoes for lunch. If the tomatoes are priced
at 4 pounds for $4.24, how much will she pay for one pound?

30. A carton of six colas sells for $4.62. How much does one cola cost?

Basic Operations with Decimals

EXAMPLES

Add.

$$\begin{array}{r} 2.3 \\ + \ 5.67 \\ \hline 7.97 \end{array}$$

Subtract.

$$\begin{array}{r} {\scriptstyle 5\ 9\ 10} \\ 3\cancel{6}.\cancel{0}\cancel{0} \\ - \ 0.93 \\ \hline 35.07 \end{array}$$

Multiply.

$$\begin{array}{r} 2.2 \\ \times \ .9 \\ \hline 1.98 \end{array}$$

Divide.

$$\begin{array}{r} .3822 \\ 9\ )\overline{3.4400} \\ -\ 27 \\ \hline 74 \\ -\ 72 \\ \hline 20 \\ -\ 18 \\ \hline 20 \\ -\ 18 \\ \hline 2 \end{array}$$

Directions Add.

1. $2.3 + 5.67 =$ _____

2. $45 + 9.97 + 0.055 =$ _____

3. $3.04 + 0.056 + 0.7 =$ _____

4. $67.3 + 34.09 + 4.45 =$ _____

5. $0.0745 + 0.45 + 0.087202 =$ _____

6. $3.45 + 0.0923 + 3.07 =$ _____

7. $2.33 + 0.76 + 74.9 + 4.4 =$ _____

8. $0.0348 + 0.2 + 4 + 4.45 =$ _____

Directions Subtract.

9. $36 - 0.93 =$ _____

10. $4.5 - 2.09 =$ _____

11. $5.943 - 0.56 =$ _____

12. $0.0982 - 0.039 =$ _____

13. $2.9 - 0.8033 =$ _____

14. $50.4 - 28.48 =$ _____

15. $1 - 0.97 =$ _____

16. $345 - 23.9 =$ _____

Directions Multiply.

17. $2.2 \times 0.9 =$ _____

18. $34 \times 5.2 =$ _____

19. $6.7 \times 0.67 =$ _____

20. $45.3 \times 0.23 =$ _____

21. $30.5 \times 4.5 =$ _____

22. $3.409 \times 0.42 =$ _____

23. $90.4 \times 2.11 =$ _____

24. $5.63 \times 0.941 =$ _____

Directions Divide. Round the quotients to the nearest hundredths.

25. $3.44 \div 9 =$ _____

26. $98.3 \div 20 =$ _____

27. $1.304 \div 1.1 =$ _____

28. $36 \div 0.7 =$ _____

29. $3 \div 1.7 =$ _____

30. $5.606 \div 25 =$ _____

Decimals to Fractions

EXAMPLE Rename 0.6 as a fraction. Simplify if necessary.

$0.6 = \frac{6}{10} = \frac{3}{5}$

Directions Rewrite each decimal as a fraction or a mixed number.
Simplify the answers to the lowest terms.

1. 0.51 = _____	**25.** 0.9 = _____	**49.** 0.353 = _____
2. 0.07 = _____	**26.** 0.102 = _____	**50.** 7.2 = _____
3. 0.5 = _____	**27.** 0.052 = _____	**51.** 0.0004 = _____
4. 0.2 = _____	**28.** 0.0071 = _____	**52.** 0.1004 = _____
5. 0.003 = _____	**29.** 0.004 = _____	**53.** 46.85 = _____
6. 0.007 = _____	**30.** 0.38 = _____	**54.** 0.999 = _____
7. 0.75 = _____	**31.** 15.1 = _____	**55.** 0.122 = _____
8. 0.82 = _____	**32.** 3.75 = _____	**56.** 0.01 = _____
9. 0.15 = _____	**33.** 0.25 = _____	**57.** 0.106 = _____
10. 1.5 = _____	**34.** 2.25 = _____	**58.** 0.004 = _____
11. 0.62 = _____	**35.** 1.82 = _____	**59.** 0.147 = _____
12. 0.085 = _____	**36.** 0.21 = _____	**60.** 54.06 = _____
13. 0.008 = _____	**37.** 1.002 = _____	**61.** 1.85 = _____
14. 0.001 = _____	**38.** 0.52 = _____	**62.** 9.43 = _____
15. 2.6 = _____	**39.** 0.42 = _____	**63.** 7.78 = _____
16. 0.022 = _____	**40.** 2.125 = _____	**64.** 4.14 = _____
17. 0.04 = _____	**41.** 0.54 = _____	**65.** 0.335 = _____
18. 20.6 = _____	**42.** 0.0085 = _____	**66.** 1.38 = _____
19. 5.03 = _____	**43.** 4.48 = _____	**67.** 0.34 = _____
20. 4.1 = _____	**44.** 1.53 = _____	**68.** 0.554 = _____
21. 200.6 = _____	**45.** 10.5 = _____	**69.** 0.332 = _____
22. 0.0012 = _____	**46.** 1.18 = _____	**70.** 0.246 = _____
23. 0.041 = _____	**47.** 24.5 = _____	
24. 0.101 = _____	**48.** 0.0002 = _____	

Fractions to Decimals

EXAMPLE   Rename $\frac{2}{3}$ as a decimal.

Round to nearest hundredth.

$$\begin{array}{r} .666 \to 0.67 \\ 3\overline{)2.000} \\ -\,1\,8 \\ \hline 20 \\ -\,18 \\ \hline 20 \\ -\,18 \\ \hline 2 \end{array}$$

Directions   Write each fraction as a decimal rounded to the nearest hundredth.

1. $\frac{1}{15}$ = _____   16. $\frac{3}{11}$ = _____   31. $\frac{2}{17}$ = _____

2. $\frac{3}{16}$ = _____   17. $\frac{1}{20}$ = _____   32. $\frac{1}{3}$ = _____

3. $\frac{1}{10}$ = _____   18. $\frac{14}{15}$ = _____   33. $\frac{2}{19}$ = _____

4. $\frac{4}{5}$ = _____   19. $\frac{2}{5}$ = _____   34. $\frac{1}{6}$ = _____

5. $\frac{1}{17}$ = _____   20. $\frac{5}{21}$ = _____   35. $\frac{3}{20}$ = _____

6. $\frac{13}{14}$ = _____   21. $\frac{3}{12}$ = _____   36. $\frac{11}{20}$ = _____

7. $\frac{6}{9}$ = _____   22. $\frac{6}{7}$ = _____   37. $\frac{9}{11}$ = _____

8. $\frac{1}{9}$ = _____   23. $\frac{3}{7}$ = _____   38. $\frac{6}{19}$ = _____

9. $\frac{9}{10}$ = _____   24. $\frac{1}{11}$ = _____   39. $\frac{7}{11}$ = _____

10. $\frac{3}{5}$ = _____   25. $\frac{1}{8}$ = _____   40. $\frac{10}{11}$ = _____

11. $\frac{5}{14}$ = _____   26. $\frac{2}{15}$ = _____   41. $\frac{5}{6}$ = _____

12. $\frac{3}{4}$ = _____   27. $\frac{15}{17}$ = _____   42. $\frac{7}{16}$ = _____

13. $\frac{1}{2}$ = _____   28. $\frac{3}{13}$ = _____   43. $\frac{5}{13}$ = _____

14. $\frac{6}{16}$ = _____   29. $\frac{3}{16}$ = _____   44. $\frac{6}{13}$ = _____

15. $\frac{11}{12}$ = _____   30. $\frac{5}{16}$ = _____   45. $\frac{8}{9}$ = _____

Changing Fractions to Decimals

EXAMPLE   Change the fraction to a decimal. Divide to 3 decimal places.
Then round to 2 places.

Hint: Try to simplify the fraction before division.

$$\frac{2}{12} = \frac{1}{6} = 6\overline{)1.000} = 0.166 = 0.17$$

Directions   Change these fractions to decimals. Divide to 3 places.
Then round to 2 places.

1. $\frac{7}{9}$ = _____   **16.** $\frac{25}{75}$ = _____

2. $\frac{5}{9}$ = _____   **17.** $\frac{50}{60}$ = _____

3. $\frac{6}{11}$ = _____   **18.** $\frac{12}{36}$ = _____

4. $\frac{7}{9}$ = _____   **19.** $\frac{12}{24}$ = _____

5. $\frac{10}{11}$ = _____   **20.** $\frac{55}{110}$ = _____

6. $\frac{11}{12}$ = _____   **21.** $\frac{35}{40}$ = _____

7. $\frac{7}{8}$ = _____   **22.** $\frac{22}{33}$ = _____

8. $\frac{12}{13}$ = _____   **23.** $\frac{7}{28}$ = _____

9. $\frac{2}{10}$ = _____   **24.** $\frac{9}{36}$ = _____

10. $\frac{4}{9}$ = _____   **25.** $\frac{20}{75}$ = _____

11. $\frac{3}{12}$ = _____   **26.** $\frac{3}{13}$ = _____

12. $\frac{2}{15}$ = _____   **27.** $\frac{17}{34}$ = _____

13. $\frac{1}{8}$ = _____   **28.** $\frac{3}{14}$ = _____

14. $\frac{1}{9}$ = _____   **29.** $\frac{5}{30}$ = _____

15. $\frac{20}{30}$ = _____   **30.** $\frac{4}{25}$ = _____

Writing Ratios

Show a ratio in its three forms.

$\frac{1}{2}$ = 1:2 = 1 to 2

Directions Express the ratios using the other two forms.

1. $\frac{4}{3}$ _____

2. 4:7 _____

3. 9 to 12 _____

4. $\frac{5}{8}$ _____

5. 12:16 _____

6. 5 to 15 _____

7. $\frac{9}{3}$ _____

8. $\frac{12}{15}$ _____

9. $\frac{16}{17}$ _____

10. $\frac{22}{11}$ _____

11. 23:80 _____

12. 3 to 7 _____

13. 4 to 9 _____

14. 5 to 18 _____

15. 26:27 _____

16. 32:42 _____

17. $\frac{34}{45}$ _____

18. 2 to 18 _____

19. 33:34 _____

20. $\frac{7}{23}$ _____

Directions Count the number of like symbols and write the ratios for each.

21. Write the ratio of the number of @'s to #'s. _____

22. Write the ratio of the number of @'s to %'s. _____

23. Write the ratio of the number of @'s to $'s. _____

24. Write the ratio of the number of @'s to *'s. _____

25. Write the ratio of the number of #'s to %'s. _____

26. Write the ratio of the number of #'s to *'s. _____

27. Write the ratio of the number of #'s to @'s. _____

28. Write the ratio of the number of *'s to @'s. _____

29. Write the ratio of the number of *'s to $'s. _____

30. Write the ratio of the number of %'s to #'s. _____

```
@ # % $ # * & $ $
# @ $ * & & # @
# @ * & & * * # @
& # @ $ $ $ $ #
@ @ $ % % & * *
& * % % $ # $ %
& * & $ # @ @ #
# $ $ % % * & * &
* & * & * * * & $ $
# # @ @ # # * *
```

Proportions

EXAMPLE   Do $\frac{7}{8}$ and $\frac{28}{32}$ form a proportion?

$\boxed{7}$ $\boxed{28}$

$\boxed{8}$ $\boxed{32}$

The cross products are both 224. The cross products are equal, so the ratios form a proportion.

$\frac{7}{8} = \frac{28}{32}$

8×28 7×32
224   224

Directions Use cross products to decide if the ratios are equal. Write an equal sign ($=$) if the ratios form a proportion. Write an inequality symbol ($\neq$) if the ratios do not form a proportion.

1. $\frac{1}{3}$ $\frac{4}{12}$

2. $\frac{15}{80}$ $\frac{4}{75}$

3. $\frac{2}{7}$ $\frac{24}{86}$

4. $\frac{108}{18}$ $\frac{18}{3}$

5. $\frac{5}{25}$ $\frac{25}{150}$

6. $\frac{2}{3}$ $\frac{9}{12}$

7. $\frac{10}{16}$ $\frac{5}{8}$

8. $\frac{7}{8}$ $\frac{15}{16}$

9. $\frac{3}{4}$ $\frac{6}{8}$

10. $\frac{5}{16}$ $\frac{25}{86}$

11. $\frac{96}{180}$ $\frac{16}{30}$

12. $\frac{2}{4}$ $\frac{4}{8}$

13. $\frac{4}{32}$ $\frac{16}{64}$

14. $\frac{9}{12}$ $\frac{27}{36}$

15. $\frac{3}{15}$ $\frac{9}{45}$

16. $\frac{72}{54}$ $\frac{9}{7}$

17. $\frac{3}{9}$ $\frac{9}{27}$

18. $\frac{1}{4}$ $\frac{2}{4}$

19. $\frac{1}{3}$ $\frac{5}{6}$

20. $\frac{4}{5}$ $\frac{20}{25}$

21. $\frac{10}{19}$ $\frac{30}{39}$

22. $\frac{3}{6}$ $\frac{5}{10}$

23. $\frac{1}{4}$ $\frac{2}{8}$

24. $\frac{5}{8}$ $\frac{3}{4}$

25. $\frac{2}{7}$ $\frac{24}{84}$

Ratios and Proportions

EXAMPLE   14 books to 2 readers

Write the ratio as a fraction. Simplify if necessary.

$$\frac{14}{2} = \frac{7}{1}$$

Directions   Write a ratio to compare each of the following. Simplify to lowest terms.

1. 12 music CD's to 4 tapes

2. 10 automobiles to 13 bikes

3. 24 apples to 8 oranges

4. 125 miles to 5 gallons of gas

5. 22 cats to 33 dogs

6. 24 baseballs to 38 players

7. 14 lb of flour to 7 shoppers

8. 8 students to 18 tables

9. 28 TV's to 56 radios

10. 22 planes to 11 trains

EXAMPLE   Cross-multiply. Divide.

$$\frac{72}{n} = \frac{8}{2}$$

$8n = 72 \times 2$ $8n = 144$ $n = 144 \div 8$

$n = 18$

Directions   Solve these proportions using the cross-product method. Express improper fractions as mixed numbers.

11. $\frac{7}{n} = \frac{14}{10}$

12. $\frac{18}{24} = \frac{2}{n}$

13. $\frac{10}{15} = \frac{25}{n}$

14. $\frac{11}{13} = \frac{n}{39}$

15. $\frac{48}{10} = \frac{n}{5}$

Basic Math Skills

Using Proportions

EXAMPLE   Cross-multiply. Compare products.

$$\overset{30}{\frac{2}{3}} \qquad \overset{33}{\frac{11}{15}} \qquad 2 \times 15 = 30 \quad 3 \times 11 = 33$$

$$\frac{2}{3} \; < \; \frac{11}{15}$$

Directions Use cross products and use $<$, $>$, or $=$ for each.

1. $\frac{12}{11}$ _____ $\frac{10}{9}$

3. $\frac{22}{40}$ _____ $\frac{20}{33}$

5. $\frac{8}{9}$ _____ $\frac{13}{15}$

2. $\frac{7}{10}$ _____ $\frac{20}{32}$

4. $\frac{8}{13}$ _____ $\frac{22}{30}$

6. $\frac{15}{21}$ _____ $\frac{17}{18}$

Directions Use the cross-product method to solve for the unknown.

7. $\frac{14}{30} = \frac{n}{90}$

9. $\frac{n}{27} = \frac{6}{9}$

11. $\frac{7}{n} = \frac{28}{56}$

8. $\frac{n}{3} = \frac{25}{12}$

10. $\frac{18}{n} = \frac{3}{12}$

12. $\frac{56}{9} = \frac{n}{4}$

Directions Write and solve proportions using the cross-product method.
Round your answers to the nearest tenths place.

13. Eldo can ride his bike 15 miles in 2 hours. How many miles can he ride in 7 hours?

14. Lacy can in-line skate 9 miles an hour. How many hours will it take her to do 30 miles?

15. Karen and Patrick worked together stringing beads for necklaces. If they can string 50 beads in 9 minutes, how long will it take for them to string 725 beads?

Meaning of Percent

<table>
<tr><td>EXAMPLE</td><td>Shade the boxes to show percent.
16% = 16 out of 100
Shade 16 boxes.</td><td></td></tr>
</table>

Directions Shade these percents.

1. 23%

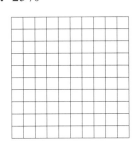

5. 33%

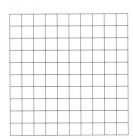

9. 95%

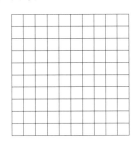

13. 55%

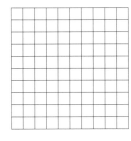

2. 75%

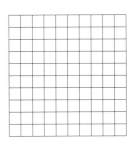

6. 80%

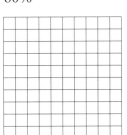

10. 45%

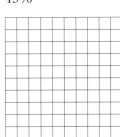

14. 12%

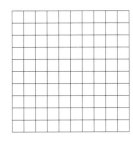

3. 30%

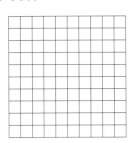

7. 9%

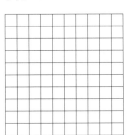

11. 60%

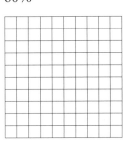

15. 68%

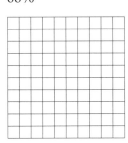

4. 40%

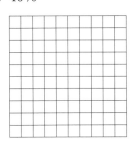

8. 17%

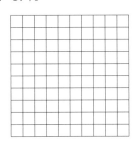

12. 100%

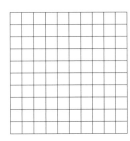

Changing Percents to Decimals and Fractions

EXAMPLES   14%   Write as a decimal. Drop percent sign. Add decimal point.
14% = 0.14

14%   Write as a fraction. Drop percent sign.
Write number as a numerator over denominator of 100.
Simplify if necessary.
$14\% = \frac{14}{100} = \frac{7}{50}$

Directions Write these percents as decimals.

1. 17% = _____

2. 33% = _____

3. 60% = _____

4. 22% = _____

5. 41% = _____

6. 46% = _____

7. 90% = _____

8. 37% = _____

9. 55% = _____

10. 75% = _____

11. 61% = _____

12. 80% = _____

13. 39% = _____

14. 66% = _____

15. 48% = _____

16. 34% = _____

17. 100% = _____

18. 1% = _____

Directions Write these decimals as fractions. Simplify your answers.

19. 0.37 = _____

20. 0.18 = _____

21. 0.11 = _____

22. 0.05 = _____

23. 0.08 = _____

24. 0.01 = _____

25. 0.33 = _____

26. 0.09 = _____

27. 0.40 = _____

28. 0.50 = _____

29. 0.68 = _____

30. 0.10 = _____

31. 0.02 = _____

32. 0.88 = _____

33. 0.25 = _____

34. 0.35 = _____

35. 0.90 = _____

36. 0.55 = _____

Directions Write these percents as decimals and fractions.
Simplify your answers.

37. 24% = _____

38. 30% = _____

39. 23% = _____

40. 33% = _____

41. 70% = _____

42. 72% = _____

43. 87% = _____

44. 95% = _____

45. 74% = _____

Decimals to Percents

EXAMPLE Rename 0.63 as a percent by moving the decimal point two places to the right and adding the percent symbol.

$0.63 = 63\%$

Directions Rewrite each decimal as a percent.

1. 0.36 = _____	**21.** 0.0045 = _____	**41.** 25.0 = _____
2. 1.35 = _____	**22.** 0.6031 = _____	**42.** 3.44 = _____
3. 0.05 = _____	**23.** 5.05 = _____	**43.** 22.332 = _____
4. 0.6 = _____	**24.** 0.2207 = _____	**44.** 5.556 = _____
5. 0.78 = _____	**25.** 0.41 = _____	**45.** 2.33 = _____
6. 0.45 = _____	**26.** 0.2246 = _____	**46.** 0.75 = _____
7. 0.0088 = _____	**27.** 0.032 = _____	**47.** 15.02 = _____
8. 0.035 = _____	**28.** 0.01 = _____	**48.** 0.0062 = _____
9. 0.122 = _____	**29.** 0.1 = _____	**49.** 30.452 = _____
10. 0.02 = _____	**30.** 0.112 = _____	**50.** 73.1 = _____
11. 0.4 = _____	**31.** 0.172 = _____	**51.** 33.4 = _____
12. 0.21 = _____	**32.** 1.75 = _____	**52.** 1.433 = _____
13. 2.09 = _____	**33.** 2 = _____	**53.** 43.14 = _____
14. 2.3 = _____	**34.** 62 = _____	**54.** 12.06 = _____
15. 6.12 = _____	**35.** 4.09 = _____	**55.** 48.045 = _____
16. 4.5 = _____	**36.** 3.1 = _____	**56.** 2.332 = _____
17. 0.065 = _____	**37.** 9.21 = _____	**57.** 2.398 = _____
18. 0.0081 = _____	**38.** 0.155 = _____	**58.** 12.124 = _____
19. 0.205 = _____	**39.** 80.0 = _____	**59.** 42.46 = _____
20. 0.244 = _____	**40.** 7.02 = _____	**60.** 0.0056 = _____

Major Elements of a Percent Sentence

EXAMPLES

	Rate	Base	Percentage
15% of what number is 52?	15%	n	52
What percent of 22 is 11?	n	22	11

Directions Identify the rate, base, and percentage for the following percent sentences. Use the letter n to represent a missing value.

	Rate	Base	Percentage
1. 56% of 90 is what number?			
2. What percent of 50 is 40?			
3. What percent of 86 is 43?			
4. 88% of 50 is what number?			
5. 100% of what number is 176?			
6. 200% of 50 is what number?			
7. 90% of what number is 64?			
8. What percent of 49 is 100?			
9. 70% of 50 is what number?			
10. 80% of 20 is what number?			
11. What percent of 120 is 90?			
12. What percent of 48 is 96?			
13. 150% of what number is 300?			
14. 6% of 33 is what number?			
15. 12% of what number is 70?			
16. What percent of 200 is 300?			
17. What percent of 5 is 30?			
18. 9% of 56 is what number?			
19. 33% of 129 is what number?			
20. 3% of what number is 27?			

Find the Percentage

EXAMPLE

8% of 20 is _____

8% of 20 is n

$0.08 \times 20 = n$

$1.6 = n$

Directions Solve for the percentage.

1. 9% of 50 is _____

2. 4% of 53 is _____

3. 28% of 4 is _____

4. 6% of 125 is _____

5. 2% of 86 is _____

6. 43% of 14 is _____

7. 75% of 92 is _____

8. 21% of 34 is _____

9. 92% of 62 is _____

10. 53% of 80 is _____

11. 15% of 28 is _____

12. 92% of 65 is _____

13. 3% of 2.1 is _____

14. 40% of 3.5 is _____

15. 7% of 0.7 is _____

16. 6% of 2.3 is _____

17. 122% of 42 is _____

18. 136% of 5 is _____

19. 200% of 73 is _____

20. 0.4% of 96 is _____

21. 7.2% of 48 is _____

22. 5.3% of 70 is _____

23. 0.8% of 245 is _____

24. 1.6% of 1.4 is _____

25. 2.8% of 9.02 is _____

26. 2.4% of 76 is _____

27. 5% of 0.083 is _____

28. 0.6% of 435 is _____

29. 0.7% of 7.49 is _____

30. 129% of 4.2 is _____

31. 0.03% of 141 is _____

32. 0.8% of 0.2 is _____

33. 0.82% of 403 is _____

34. 245% of 2.6 is _____

35. 10% of 45 is _____

36. 3.4% of 500 is _____

37. 45% of 100 is _____

38. 23.4% of 300 is _____

39. 140% of 62 is _____

40. 7% of 250 is _____

41. 0.46% of 746 is _____

42. 6.5% of 30 is _____

43. 7.9% of 500 is _____

44. 200% of 0.33 is _____

45. 9% of 9 is _____

Find the Base

EXAMPLE 5% of _____ is 1.4

5% of n is 1.4
$$0.05 \times n = 1.4$$
$$n = 1.4 \div 0.05$$
$$n = 28$$

$$
\begin{array}{r}
28 \\
0.5\overline{)1.40} \\
-1\,0 \\
\hline
40 \\
-40 \\
\hline
\end{array}
$$

Directions Solve for the base.

1. 5% of _____ is 4.1

2. 2% of _____ is 3.6

3. 6% of _____ is 1.8

4. 3% of _____ is 0.27

5. 7% of _____ is 0.196

6. 4% of _____ is 1.28

7. 50% of _____ is 2.7

8. 35% of _____ is 30.8

9. 6% of _____ is 0.078

10. 8% of _____ is 0.32

11. 2.5% of _____ is 0.15

12. 7.3% of _____ is 2.044

13. 120% of _____ is 50.4

14. 3.4% of _____ is 2.38

15. 9% of _____ is 0.315

16. 5% of _____ is 0.13

17. 5% of _____ is 0.0235

18. 41% of _____ is 0.82

19. 3% of _____ is 0.045

20. 245% of _____ is 191.1

21. 9% of _____ is 0.0594

22. 0.3% of _____ is 0.135

23. 0.75% of _____ is 0.9

24. 0.8% of _____ is 0.4

25. 4% of _____ is 0.0176

26. 0.21% of _____ is 0.0735

27. 150% of _____ is 135

28. 125% of _____ is 62.5

29. 5.2% of _____ is 0.0988

30. 3.4% of _____ is 0.3094

31. 0.5% of _____ is 1.19

32. 0.21% of _____ is 0.0147

33. 0.32% of _____ is 0.32

34. 0.75% of _____ is 7.5

35. 8% of _____ is 0.416

36. 1.4% of _____ is 0.196

37. 6% of _____ is 0.138

38. 5% of _____ is 0.115

39. 120% of _____ is 102

40. 1% of _____ is 0.03

41. 0.9% of _____ is 1.35

42. 6.3% of _____ is 0.252

43. 8% of _____ is 16

44. 4% of _____ is 0.024

45. 1.6% of _____ is 3.376

Find the Rate

EXAMPLE _____% of 80 is 4.8

n% of 80 is 4.8

$\quad n \times 0.80 = 4.8$

$\qquad n = 4.8 \div 0.80$

$\qquad n = 6\%$

$$0.80\overline{)4.8} \atop {\underline{-48} \atop 0}$$ 6

or

$n \times 80 = 4.8$

$n = \dfrac{4.8}{80}$

$n = 0.06 = 6\%$

Directions Solve for the rate.

1. _____ % of 25 is 5

2. _____ % of 35 is 1.05

3. _____ % of 70 is 3.5

4. _____ % of 30 is 1.8

5. _____ % of 80 is 5.6

6. _____ % of 20 is 1.8

7. _____ % of 80 is 0.56

8. _____ % of 200 is 102

9. _____ % of 20 is 7

10. _____ % of 300 is 45

11. _____ % of 100 is 9

12. _____ % of 2,000 is 360

13. _____ % of 35 is 2.8

14. _____ % of 305 is 48.8

15. _____ % of 20 is 30

16. _____ % of 64 is 112

17. _____ % of 10.5 is 0.84

18. _____ % of 250 is 70

19. _____ % of 38 is 1.14

20. _____ % of 72 is 1.08

21. _____ % of 206 is 16.48

22. _____ % of 500 is 4.5

23. _____ % of 2.06 is 0.1442

24. _____ % of 600 is 420

25. _____ % of 700 is 9.8

26. _____ % of 40 is 0.32

27. _____ % of 200 is 0.14

28. _____ % of 3,000 is 1.8

29. _____ % of 2.5 is 0.9

30. _____ % of 4.2 is 0.546

31. _____ % of 4 is 0.12

32. _____ % of 400 is 0.08

33. _____ % of 22 is 56.1

34. _____ % of 30 is 106.5

35. _____ % of 80 is 14

36. _____ % of 15 is 0.56

37. _____ % of 90 is 5.4

38. _____ % of 50 is 100

39. _____ % of 23 is 2.3

40. _____ % of 120 is 300

41. _____ % of 22 is 0.33

42. _____ % of 30 is 2.85

43. _____ % of 70 is 4.9

44. _____ % of 0.16 is 0.000136

45. _____ % of 50 is 9

Percent Sentences

EXAMPLES

Percentage	Base	Rate
25% of 80 is _____	25% of _____ is 52	_____% of 44 is 11
$25\% \times 80 = n$	$25\% \times n = 52$	$n\% \times 44 = 11$
$0.25 \times 80 = 20$	$0.25n = 52$	$n \times 0.44 = 11$
	$n = 208$	$n = 11 \div 0.44$
		$n = 25\%$

Directions Solve for the percentage.

1. 25% of 60 is   _____

2. 82% of 50 is   _____

3. 90% of 60 is   _____

4. 35% of 36 is   _____

5. 92% of 100 is   _____

6. 20% of 30 is   _____

Directions Solve for the base.

7. 15% of _____ is 9

8. 60% of _____ is 15

9. 20% of _____ is 8

10. 62% of _____ is 10.54

11. 53% of _____ is 106

12. 92% of _____ is 23

Directions Solve for the rate.

13. _____ % of 9.5 is 7.6

14. _____ % of 70 is 21

15. _____ % of 45 is 4.05

16. _____ % of 30 is 21

17. _____ % of 80 is 72

18. _____ % of 26 is 0.65

Directions Complete each percent sentence.

19. _____ % of 2.5 is 0.375

20. 5.5% of _____ is 0.2475

21. 0.5% of 75 is _____

22. 2.8% of _____ is 18.2

23. _____ % of 240 is 192

24. 75% of _____ is 225

25. 10% of _____ is 0.26

Using Proportions

EXAMPLES

Find base.	Find rate.	Find percentage.
25% of n is 17.5	n% of 40 is 24	7% of 80 is n
$\frac{25}{100} = \frac{17.5}{n}$	$\frac{n}{100} = \frac{24}{40}$	$\frac{7}{100} = \frac{n}{80}$
$100 \times 17.5 = 25n$	$100 \times 24 = 40n$	$100n = 7 \times 80$
$1{,}750 = 25n$	$2{,}400 = 40n$	$100n = 560$
$\frac{1{,}750}{25} = \frac{25n}{25}$	$\frac{2{,}400}{40} = \frac{40n}{40}$	$\frac{100n}{100} = \frac{560}{100}$
$70 = n$	$60 = n$	$n = 5.6$

Directions Write proportions and solve for the unknown.

1. 20% of n is 9.6 _____

2. n% of 35 is 5.6 _____

3. 70% of 32 is n _____

4. 30% of n is 120 _____

5. n% of 50 is 11.5 _____

6. 85% of 36 is n _____

7. 90% of n is 270 _____

8. n% of 97 is 48.5 _____

9. 80% of 40 is n _____

10. 23% of n is 73.6 _____

11. n% of 60 is 24 _____

12. 35% of n is 24.5 _____

13. 18% of 350 is n _____

14. n% of 29 is 2.03 _____

15. 9% of n is 4.68 _____

Discount

EXAMPLES Find the sale price of a music CD that lists for $18.50, if the discount rate is 20%.

Step 1 $18.50 list price
          × .20
          $3.70 discount

Step 2 $18.50 list price
          − 3.70 discount
          $14.80 price after discount

Find the discount rate if a $25.00 DVD is on sale for $21.25.

Step 1 $25.00 list price
          − 21.25 discount price
          $3.75   discount

$$.15 = 15\% \text{ discount rate}$$
$$25\overline{)3.75}$$
$$- 2\,5$$
$$125$$
$$- 125$$

Directions Solve these discount problems. When necessary round answers to the nearest cent.

1. $175.00 list price
10% discount rate

Discount _____

Sale price _____

2. $80.00 list price
20% discount rate

Discount _____

Sale price _____

3. CD list price $22.00
15% discount rate

Discount _____

Sale price _____

4. Videotape list price $50.00
Sale price $20.00

Discount _____

Discount rate _____

5. Computer list price $950.00
Discount rate 10%

Discount _____

Sale price _____

6. Radio list price $75.00
Discount rate 15%

Discount _____

Sale price _____

7. Stereo list price $150.00
Sale price $120.00

Discount _____

Discount rate _____

8. Disk drive list price $150.00
Discount rate 20%

Discount _____

Sale price _____

9. Television list price $395.00
Discount rate 10%

Discount _____

Sale price _____

10. Jeans list price $34.95
Discount rate 10%

Discount _____

Sale price _____

Sales Tax

EXAMPLE   Compute 6% sales tax on $13.05

$13.05 cost before tax

$\underline{\times\quad .06}$ tax rate

0.7830

0.79 ◄─────── Tax **always** rounds up.

The tax is $0.79 or 79 cents.

Directions Compute sales tax.

1. $2.75 at 5% _____

2. $6.15 at 7% _____

3. $24.95 at 7% _____

4. $120.00 at 5% _____

5. $1,200.00 at 6% _____

6. $16.75 at 6% _____

7. $100.00 at 6% _____

8. $30.10 at 7% _____

9. $0.45 at 5% _____

Directions Compute sales tax and total cost.

10. A book for $17.95

6% tax rate

Tax _____

Cost plus tax _____

11. Clock for $75.00

5% tax rate

Tax _____

Cost plus tax _____

12. Television for $299.99

7% tax rate

Tax _____

Cost plus tax _____

13. Table for $98.00

5% tax rate

Tax _____

Cost plus tax _____

14. Used car for $11,960.00

6% tax rate

Tax _____

Cost plus tax _____

15. Electric stove for $699.00

5% tax rate

Tax _____

Cost plus tax _____

Simple Interest

EXAMPLE   Compute the simple interest on a principal of $125.00 at an interest rate of 7% for 3 years.

     $125.00   principal $8.75   interest for one year

     $\times$ .07 $\times$ 3   for 3 years

     $8.7500   interest for one year $26.25   interest for 3 years

Compute the simple interest on $200.00 at a rate of 6% for 9 months.

     $200.00   principal $\dfrac{\$12}{1} \times \dfrac{9}{12}$ ←   Write 9 months over 12

     $\times$ .06   months to express time

      $12.00   interest for 1 year $\dfrac{12}{1} \times \dfrac{3}{4} = \dfrac{36}{4} = 9$ as years.

     $9.00 is the interest for 9 months.

Directions   Compute the simple interest.

1. Compute the simple interest for $750.00 at 7% for 5 years.   _____

2. Compute the simple interest for $800.00 at 6% for 6 months.   _____

3. Compute the simple interest for $1,200.00 at 9% for 10 years.   _____

4. Compute the simple interest for $5,000.00 at 10% for 5 years.   _____

5. Compute the simple interest for $6,200.00 at 8% for 10 years.   _____

6. Compute the simple interest for $150.00 at 5% for 11 years.   _____

7. Compute the simple interest for $48.00 at 5% for 6 months.   _____

8. Compute the simple interest for $4,500.00 at 7% for 9 months. _____

9. Compute the simple interest for $395.00 at 3% for 24 months.   _____

10. Compute the simple interest for $245.00 at 5% for 7 years.   _____

Installment Buying

EXAMPLE Find the finance charge and balance with a 2% finance rate for $400.00.

Step 1 $400.00   previous balance   **Step 2** $400.00   previous balance
         $\times$ .02   finance rate   +   8.00   finance charge

         $8.0000   finance charge $408.00

New balance before first payment

Step 3 $408.00
        −   25.00   first month's payment

        $383.00   new balance

Directions Complete the installment chart for a TV that cost $400.00. The monthly payments will be $25.00 and a 2% finance charge will be added to the unpaid balance.

Month	Previous Balance	Finance Charge	Before Payment	Monthly Payment	New Balance
June	$400.00	$8.00	$408.00	$25.00	$383.00
July	$383.00				
August					
September					
October					

Directions Complete the installment chart for a TV that cost $400.00 with a 1% finance charge added to the unpaid balance. The monthly payments are $25.00.

Month	Previous Balance	Finance Charge	Before Payment	Monthly Payment	New Balance
June					
July					
August					
September					
October					

Commission

EXAMPLE   Compute the commission for a real estate agent who sells a house
for $95,000 and the commission rate is 3%.

$95,000.00 sale price
×   .03 commission rate
$2,850.00 commission

Directions Compute the following sales commissions.

1. Amount is $4,500.00

Commission rate 5%

Commission _____

2. Amount is $48,000.00

Commission rate 3%

Commission _____

3. Amount is $3,400.00

Commission rate 3%

Commission _____

4. Amount is $500.00

Commission rate 5%

Commission _____

5. Amount is $1,000.00

Commission rate 3%

Commission _____

6. Amount is $1,600.00

Commission rate 3%

Commission _____

7. Amount is $450.00

Commission rate 5%

Commission _____

8. Amount is $1,700.00

Commission rate 4%

Commission _____

9. Amount is $3,400.00

Commission rate 5%

Commission _____

10. Amount is $950.00

Commission rate 10%

Commission _____

11. Amount is $560.00

Commission rate 5%

Commission _____

12. Amount is $880.00

Commission rate 4%

Commission _____

13. Amount is $234.00

Commission rate 11%

Commission _____

14. Amount is $911.00

Commission rate 4%

Commission _____

15. Amount is $260.00

Commission rate 9%

Commission _____

Tips

EXAMPLE | Compute a 15% tip on a meal that costs $23.50.

$23.50 meal cost $23.50 meal cost
×   .15 tip rate   × 3.53 tip
  11750 $27.03 total
   2350
$3.5250 round to nearest cent

$3.53 rounded to nearest cent

Directions Compute the tip for each meal. Use 15% as a tip rate for each meal.

1. Meal cost $20.00

Tip _____

Meal total _____

4. Meal cost $25.00

Tip _____

Meal total _____

7. Meal cost $5.50

Tip _____

Meal total _____

2. Meal cost $27.20

Tip _____

Meal total _____

5. Meal cost $45.20

Tip _____

Meal total _____

8. Meal cost $11.90

Tip _____

Meal total _____

3. Meal cost $37.00

Tip _____

Meal total _____

6. Meal cost $18.00

Tip _____

Meal total _____

9. Meal cost $4.50

Tip _____

Meal total _____

Directions Compute the tip for each meal and round to the nearest dollar.

10. Meal cost $4.60

Tip _____

Meal total _____

12. Meal cost $11.90

Tip _____

Meal total _____

14. Meal cost $5.50

Tip _____

Meal total _____

11. Meal cost $15.50

Tip _____

Meal total _____

13. Meal cost $14.70

Tip _____

Meal total _____

15. Meal cost $7.95

Tip _____

Meal total _____

Points, Lines, and Angles

EXAMPLE   Make a construction to represent $\overrightarrow{AB}$.

A   B   B   A
●──────────●──▶   ◀──────●──────────●

Rays can be drawn from either direction.
The beginning point must be A as indicated $\overrightarrow{AB}$.

Directions Use the baseline provided to construct the following
geometric constructions.

1. $\overrightarrow{BA}$ _____

2. $\angle ABC$ _____

3. $\angle XYZ$ _____

4. $\overrightarrow{AD}$ _____

5. $\overline{DZ}$ _____

6. Vertex G _____

7. Vertex H _____

8. $\overleftrightarrow{RT}$ _____

9. point B _____

10. $\angle QRS$ _____

Identifying Angles

Construct an acute angle.

∠*ABC* is acute because ∠*B*
is less than 90 degrees.

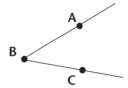

Directions Construct these angles on the baselines given.

1. acute   **4.** reflex

_____   _____

2. straight   **5.** right

_____   _____

3. obtuse

_____

Measuring Angles

EXAMPLE

Place protractor on the angle so that the center is on the angle's vertex and the baseline is on one of the rays.

Make sure second ray crosses the scale. Read the scale.

_45°_

Directions Use a protractor to measure these angles to the nearest degree. If necessary, use a straightedge to extend the sides of the angle.

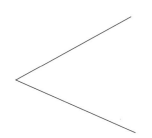

1. _____

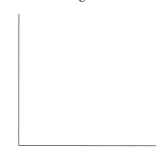

4. _____

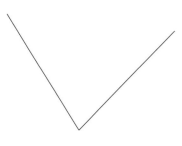

2. _____

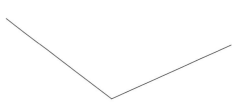

5. _____

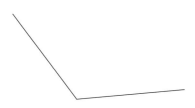

3. _____

Polygons

Count the number of sides. Name the polygon.

_____quadrilateral_____

Directions Count the number of sides for each polygon. Use the chart to classify each polygon.

1.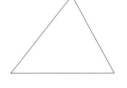

_____

2.

_____

3.

_____

4.

_____

5.

_____

6.

_____

7.

_____

8.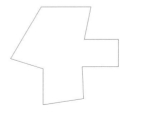

_____

Number of Sides	Name of Polygon
3	triangle
4	quadrilateral
5	pentagon
6	hexagon
7	heptagon
8	octagon
9	nonagon
10	decagon
12	dodecagon

9.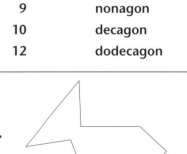

_____

10.

_____

Solid Figures

EXAMPLE   Look at the solid figure. Identify it.

       _____cone_____

Directions Identify these solid figures.

1.

_____

2.

_____

3.

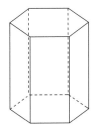

_____

4.

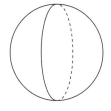

_____

5.

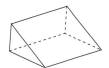

_____

6.

_____

7.

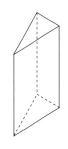

_____

8.

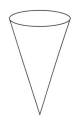

_____

9.

_____

10.

_____

Units of Measurement

EXAMPLE   Circle the letter of the best answer. Think about the meaning of the prefix.
Convert from one unit of measurement to the other.

4 centimeters
A 0.004 meter
Ⓑ 0.04 meter   *Centi* means one-hundredth. 4 centimeters is 4
C 0.40 meter   one-hundredths, or 0.04, meters.
D 4 meter

Directions Circle the letter of the best answer.

1. 3 millimeters
   A 3 meters
   B 30 meters
   C 0.03 meters
   D 0.003 meters

2. 7 kilometers
   A 70 meters
   B 700 meters
   C 7,000 meters
   D 0.007 meters

Prefix	Value	Symbol	Example
kilo	one thousand	k	kilometer
hecto	one hundred	h	hectometer
deka	ten	da	dekagram
deci	one-tenth	d	decimeter
centi	one-hundredth	c	centigram
milli	one-thousandth	m	milliliter

Sometimes **deka** is spelled **deca**.

3. 8 centimeters
   A 0.08 meters
   B 0.8 meters
   C 80 meters
   D 8 meters

6. 3 decimeters
   A 3 meters
   B 0.3 meters
   C 0.03 meters
   D 30 meters

9. 7 decimeters
   A 0.7 meters
   B 0.07 meters
   C 70 meters
   D 700 meters

4. 9 dekameters
   A 9 meters
   B 90 meters
   C 0.09 meters
   D 900 meters

7. 19 kilometers
   A 190 meters
   B 0.0019 meters
   C 1,900 meters
   D 19,000 meters

10. 3,000 millimeters
   A 300 meters
   B 30 meters
   C 3 meters
   D 0.03 meters

5. 4 hectometers
   A 40 meters
   B 0.04 meters
   C 0.004 meters
   D 400 meters

8. 27 centimeters
   A 2.7 meters
   B 0.27 meters
   C 0.027 meters
   D 27 meters

Name Date Period

Workbook Activity 90

Chapter 8, Lesson 2

Using the Metric System

EXAMPLE Use a metric ruler to measure the line to the nearest millimeter.

Give your answer in centimeters and millimeters.

7 cm 4 mm

Directions Measure these line segments using the metric system. Measure to the nearest millimeter. Write your answers on the line.

1. ____________________

2. ____________________

3. ____________________

4. ____________________

5. ____________________

6. ____________________

7. ____________________

8. ____________________

9. ____________________

10. ____________________

11. ____________________

12. ____________________

13. ____________________

14. ____________________

15. ____________________

Converting Units

EXAMPLES

4.5 m = ___450___ cm   km _3_ m _2_ cm _1_ mm
2 places ⟶   ⟶

6.2 cm = ___0.000062___ km   km _3_ m _2_ cm _1_ mm
       ⟵ 5 places   ⟵

The decimal has moved 5 places to the left. Also note that the
arrow has moved under the 2 and the 3. 2 + 3 = 5
Move the decimal 5 places in the direction of the arrow.

Directions Make the following conversions.

1. 5 m = _____ mm

2. 2 cm = _____ mm

┌─────────────────────────────────────┐
│ 1 kilometer = 1,000 meters   │
│ 1 meter = 100 centimeters   │
│ 1 meter = 1,000 millimeters   │
│ 1 centimeter = 10 millimeters   │
└─────────────────────────────────────┘

3. 12 km = _____ m

4. 9 cm = _____ m   **11.** 29,000 mm = _____ m

5. 2.3 cm = _____ m   **12.** 9,000,000 mm = _____ km

6. 3.44 km = _____ cm   **13.** 0.0003 cm = _____ km

7. 19 mm = _____ cm   **14.** 0.004 cm = _____ mm

8. 7.1 cm = _____ km   **15.** 82 mm = _____ m

9. 2 cm = _____ m

10. 0.04 km = _____ m

Working with Measurements of Length

EXAMPLE   Add. Convert meters to centimeters.

2 m + 350 cm

200 m + 350 cm = 550 cm

Directions Use the charts to help make these conversions.

1. 234 mm = _____ cm

2. 82 m = _____ km

3. 3.4 mm = _____ m

4. 5 km = _____ cm

km	_3_	m	_2_	cm	_1_	mm

1 kilometer = 1,000 meters

1 meter = 100 centimeters

1 meter = 1,000 millimeters

1 centimeter = 10 millimeters

5. 35 cm = _____ mm

6. 87 mm = _____ km

7. 3.2 cm = _____ mm

8. 0.24 km = _____ m

9. 0.7 mm = _____ cm

10. 0.001 km = _____ m

11. 15 cm = _____ m

12. 0.02 m = _____ cm

Directions Find the answers to these addition problems.

13. 34 cm + 4.9 cm + 7 cm = _____ cm

14. 9 mm + 22 mm = _____ mm

15. 66 m + 120 cm + 10 m = _____ m

16. 4 km + 5 m + 120 cm = _____ m

17. 3.4 cm + 12 mm + 4 mm = _____ mm

18. 2 km + 23 m + 300 cm = _____ m

19. 4 m + 34 m + 0.005 km = _____ m

20. 1 cm + 1 m = _____ m

21. 9 mm + 30 mm + 1.1 cm = _____ mm

22. 8 km + 2,031 m = _____ km

23. 30 m + 20 cm = _____ km

24. 0.003 km + 2 m = _____ cm

25. 4 mm + 30 cm = _____ mm

Computing Area of a Rectangle

EXAMPLE

Area = length × width

Area = 4 units × 2 units

Area = 8 square units

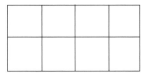

4 units

2 units

Directions Solve for the area of these rectangles.

1.

2 meters

4 meters

_____

2.

25 cm

20 cm

_____

3.

10 cm

19 cm

_____

4.

11 meters

8 meters

_____

5.

56 m

13 m

_____

6.

10 cm

39 cm

_____

7.

9 km

22 km

_____

8.

23 mm

78 mm

_____

9.

20 mm

10 mm

_____

10.

9 cm

30 cm

_____

Computing Volume

EXAMPLE   Compute the volume for this rectangular prism.

Volume = length × width × height

Volume = 10 cm × 8 cm × 9 cm

Volume = 720 cubic cm

All volume measurements are expressed in cubic units.

Directions Compute the volumes.

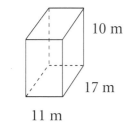

1. 10 m 17 m 11 m

_____

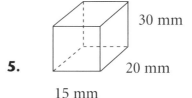

5. 30 mm 20 mm 15 mm

_____

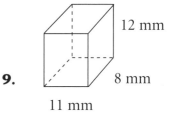

9. 12 mm 8 mm 11 mm

_____

2. length = 1 km
width = 2 km
height = 5 km

_____

6. length = 12 cm
width = 20 cm
height = 6 cm

_____

10. length = 45 cm
width = 17 cm
height = 10 cm

_____

3. length = 13 cm
width = 8 cm
height = 20 cm

_____

7. length = 100 m
width = 100 m
height = 10 m

_____

4. length = 22 km
width = 22 km
height = 10 km

_____

8. length = 25 km
width = 20 km
height = 40 km

_____

Capacity

EXAMPLE   Capacity is the amount a container will hold when full.

Liter is L. The L is always capitalized in abbreviations.

Centiliter is cL, kiloliter is kL, and milliliter is mL.

15 L = _____ cL

1 L = 100 cL, so

15 L = 1,500 cL

| 1 kiloliter = 1,000 liters |
| 1 liter = 100 centiliters |
| 1 centiliter = 10 milliliters |

Directions Choose the proper unit of measure for each of these examples.

1. a large container of milk

_____

2. the amount of water in a swimming pool

_____

3. the amount of cream in a bowl

_____

4. milk shake in a paper cup

_____

5. trunk space of a large car

_____

6. automobile gas tank

_____

7. the amount of salt needed

_____

8. a bottle of perfume

_____

9. a thimble full of water

_____

10. a bathtub full of water

_____

Directions Make these conversions using the table.

11. 2 kiloliters = _____ liters

12. 2,000 liters = _____ kiloliters

13. 300 milliliters = _____ cL

14. 400 mL = _____ liters

15. 9 kL = _____ L

16. 200 centiliters = _____ milliliters

17. 1 kL = _____ L

18. 30 mL = _____ centiliters

19. 10 L = _____ cL

20. 40 cL = _____ mL

Units of Capacity

EXAMPLE   kL __3__ L __2__ cL __1__ mL

2,200 mL = _____ L

1,000 mL = 1 L, so

2,200 mL = __2.2__ L

> 1 kiloliter = 1,000 liters
>
> 1 liter = 100 centiliters
>
> 1 centiliter = 10 milliliters
>
> 1 liter = 1,000 milliliters

Directions Use these charts to help determine the correct conversion.

1. 4,500 mL = _____ L

2. 0.00012 kL = _____ L

3. 2.3 L = _____ mL

4. 3.6 L = _____ kL

5. 0.091 mL = _____ cL

6. 7 mL = _____ L

Directions Solve for the volumes.

7. length = 2 mm
width = 3 mm
height = 4 mm
volume = _____ mm^3

8. length = 8 cm
width = 5 cm
height = 9 cm
volume = _____ cm^3

9. length = 12 m
width = 4 m
height = 1 m
volume = _____ m^3

10. length = 1 m
width = 1 m
height = 50 cm
volume = _____ cm^3

11. length = 4 mm
width = 20 mm
height = 1 cm
volume = _____ mm^3

12. length = 2.3 cm
width = 100 cm
height = 20 mm
volume = _____ cm^3

13. length = 3 km
width = 10 km
height = 1 km
volume = _____ km^3

14. length = 90 cm
width = 300 cm
height = 1 m
volume = _____ cm^3

15. length = 45 mm
width = 2 cm
height = 20 cm
volume = _____ cm^3

Mass

  EXAMPLE   Circle the best measurement.

a bag of flour

mg   g   (kg)

A bag of flour weighs more than 1,000 grams, so use kilograms to measure its mass.

Directions   Choose the best measurement for each of these items. Circle your answer.

1. a pencil

mg   g   kg

2. a grape

mg   g   kg

3. a sunflower seed

mg   g   kg

4. a small child

mg   g   kg

5. an automobile

mg   g   kg

6. a soup bowl

mg   g   kg

7. a textbook

mg   g   kg

8. a tube of toothpaste

mg   g   kg

9. a box of cereal

mg   g   kg

10. an apple

mg   g   kg

11. a toothpick

mg   g   kg

12. one large steak

mg   g   kg

13. a large cow

mg   g   kg

14. a small cow

mg   g   kg

15. a sheep

mg   g   kg

16. a 17-inch TV

mg   g   kg

17. a sandwich

mg   g   kg

18. a tomato

mg   g   kg

19. a can of soup

mg   g   kg

20. a kitchen table

mg   g   kg

21. a large turkey

mg   g   kg

22. a ballpoint pen

mg   g   kg

23. a plate full of chicken

mg   g   kg

24. one large shoe

mg   g   kg

25. one carrot

mg   g   kg

26. an egg sandwich

mg   g   kg

27. a bike

mg   g   kg

28. one peanut

mg   g   kg

29. one grain of salt

mg   g   kg

30. a train

mg   g   kg

Working with Units of Mass

EXAMPLE   3,400 grams _____ kilograms

kg _3_ g _2_ cg _1_ mg

Step 1 Draw a line from g to kg.

Step 2 The line moves to the left as it passes the 3.

3,400 grams   Move the decimal 3 places to the left.

3,400 grams __3.4__ kilograms

Directions Use the chart to help make the conversions.

1. 23 mg = _____ g

2. 31 mg = _____ g

3. 32 g = _____ kg

1 kilogram = 1,000 grams
1 gram = 100 centigrams
1 centigram = 10 milligrams
1 gram = 1,000 milligrams

4. 120 cg = _____ g

10. 1 kg = _____ cg

5. 13 kg = _____ cg

11. 1,000 cg = _____ g

6. 350 kg = _____ g

12. 300 g = _____ kg

7. 100 mg = _____ g

13. 20 g = _____ cg

8. 300 mg = _____ cg

14. 50 mg = _____ kg

9. 240 cg = _____ g

15. 1,500 g = _____ kg

Liquid Capacity

EXAMPLES If necessary, change the units to intermediate units first.

10 quarts = _____ fluid ounces
Write this:
10 quarts = __20__ pints = __320__ fluid ounces

6 pints = __96__ fluid ounces
Multiply. 6 × 16 = 96

Commonly Used Measurements
1 pint = 16 fluid ounces
1 quart = 2 pints
1 quart = 32 fluid ounces
1 gallon = 4 quarts

Directions Make these conversions. Multiply when you are converting
from large to smaller units.

1. 2 quarts = _____ pints

2. 4 quarts = _____ pints

3. 4 gallons = _____ quarts

4. 3 pints = _____ fluid ounces

5. 5 quarts = _____ pints

6. 2 gallons = _____ quarts

7. 5 pints = _____ fluid ounces

8. 10 gallons = _____ quarts

9. 20 quarts = _____ pints

10. 13 quarts = _____ pints

11. 20 quarts = _____ fluid ounces

12. 3 gallons = _____ pints

13. 4 quarts = _____ fluid ounces

Directions Make these conversions. Divide when you are converting from small
to larger units. If necessary express answers as mixed numbers.

14. 40 pints = _____ quarts

15. 14 quarts = _____ gallons

16. 48 fluid ounces = _____ pints

17. 22 pints = _____ quarts

18. 32 pints = _____ quarts

19. 30 quarts = _____ gallons

20. 12 pints = _____ quarts

21. 34 quarts = _____ gallons

22. 45 fluid ounces = _____ pints

23. 80 quarts = _____ gallons

24. 56 fluid ounces = _____ pints

25. 23 pints = _____ quarts

Converting Units of Weight

EXAMPLES Multiply or divide to convert units.

2 tons = _____ pounds

2 × 2,000 = 4,000 pounds

3,000 pounds = _____ tons

$3,000 ÷ 2,000 = 1\frac{1}{2}$ tons

Commonly Used Measurements
1 pound = 16 ounces
1 ton = 2,000 pounds

Directions Multiply to convert large units to smaller units.

1. 3 tons = _____ pounds

2. 5.5 pounds = _____ ounces

3. 10 pounds = _____ ounces

4. 7 tons = _____ pounds

5. 7 pounds = _____ ounces

6. 4.5 tons = _____ pounds

7. 2.5 pounds = _____ ounces

8. 32 pounds = _____ ounces

9. 5 tons = _____ ounces

10. 11 pounds = _____ ounces

11. 15 tons = _____ pounds

12. 2.5 pounds = _____ ounces

13. 1.5 pounds = _____ ounces

14. 1.5 tons = _____ pounds

Directions Divide to convert small units to larger units. Some
remainders may be expressed as fractions.

15. 40,000 pounds = _____ tons

16. 48 ounces = _____ pounds

17. 64,000 ounces = _____ pounds

18. 32 ounces = _____ pounds

19. 21,000 pounds = _____ tons

20. 550 ounces = _____ pounds

21. 100 ounces = _____ pounds

22. 4,500 pounds = _____ tons

23. 35,000 pounds = _____ tons

24. 4,600 pounds = _____ tons

25. 8,800 pounds = _____ tons

Measuring Lengths

EXAMPLE   Use a ruler to measure the length.

Draw a vertical rule. Label it *B*.

$\overline{AB}$ = 3 inches   *A* _____ *B*

Directions   Use a ruler to mark the following measurements. Begin the measured line with point *A* ending with point *B*.

1. $\overline{AB}$ = 2 inches   *A* _____

2. $\overline{AB}$ = 3.5 inches   *A* _____

3. $\overline{AB}$ = $2\frac{1}{2}$ inches   *A* _____

4. $\overline{AB}$ = 4 inches   *A* _____

5. $\overline{AB}$ = $2\frac{1}{8}$ inches   *A* _____

6. $\overline{AB}$ = $3\frac{1}{4}$ inches   *A* _____

7. $\overline{AB}$ = 3.75 inches   *A* _____

8. $\overline{AB}$ = $1\frac{1}{4}$ inches   *A* _____

9. $\overline{AB}$ = $1\frac{1}{2}$ inches   *A* _____

10. $\overline{AB}$ = $1\frac{7}{8}$ inches   *A* _____

11. $\overline{AB}$ = $2\frac{4}{8}$ inches   *A* _____

12. $\overline{AB}$ = $1\frac{15}{16}$ inches   *A* _____

13. $\overline{AB}$ = 4.5 inches   *A* _____

14. $\overline{AB}$ = $2\frac{5}{8}$ inches   *A* _____

Directions   Measure the lengths of these lines to the nearest $\frac{1}{4}$ inch.

15. _____

16. _____

17. _____

18. _____

19. _____

20. _____

Length and Distances

EXAMPLES   Use the chart below to make conversions.

4 feet = _____ inches   120 inches = _____ feet

4 × 12 = 48   120 ÷ 12 = 10

↙ 12 inches = 1 foot   ↙ 12 inches = 1 foot

4 feet = __48__ inches   120 inches = __10__ feet

Directions Use the chart and multiply to make these conversions.

1. 5 feet = _____ inches

2. 5 yards = _____ feet

3. 2 miles = _____ feet

4. 8 feet = _____ inches

5. 4 yards = _____ inches

6. 56 yards = _____ feet

7. 9 feet = _____ inches

8. 7 miles = _____ inches

1 foot = 12 inches
1 yard = 36 inches
1 yard = 3 feet
1 mile = 5,280 feet

9. 20 feet = _____ inches

10. 7 feet = _____ inches

11. 36 yards = _____ inches

12. 10 miles = _____ feet

Directions Use the chart and divide to make these conversions.
Express any remainders as fractions.

13. 180 inches = _____ feet

14. 38 inches = _____ feet

15. 96 inches = _____ feet

16. 39 inches = _____ feet

17. 50 inches = _____ feet

18. 52 feet = _____ yards

19. 15,840 feet = _____ miles

20. 75 feet = _____ yards

21. 21,120 feet = _____ miles

22. 300 feet = _____ yards

23. 6,000 feet = _____ miles

24. 192 inches = _____ feet

25. 288 inches = _____ yards

Operations with Linear Measurements

EXAMPLES   Add.   Subtract.   Multiply.   Divide.

3 feet 5 inches	$\overset{5}{\cancel{6}}$ feet $\overset{17}{\cancel{8}}$ inches	2 feet 3 inches	12 yards 6 feet 10 inches ÷ 2 =
+ 7 feet 9 inches	− 2 feet 9 inches	× 6	$\frac{12\text{ yards}}{2}$ $\frac{6\text{ feet}}{2}$ $\frac{10\text{ inches}}{2}$ =
10 feet 14 inches	3 feet 8 inches	12 feet 18 inches	
or		or	6 yards 3 feet 5 inches
11 feet 2 inches		13 feet 6 inches	

Directions Add these units of measure and simplify answers.

1. 4 yards 3 feet
   + 2 yards 4 feet

2. 8 feet 11 inches
   + 2 feet   5 inches

3. 5 feet 6 inches + 6 feet 2 inches

4. 7 yards 6 feet + 4 yards 6 feet

5. 6 yards 11 inches + 5 yards 9 inches

Directions Subtract these units of measure. Simplify the answers.

6. 12 yards 2 feet
   − 3 yards 3 feet

7. 9 feet 11 inches
   − 2 feet   9 inches

8. 2 yards 2 feet − 4 feet = _____

9. 8 feet 6 inches − 3 feet 9 inches = _____

10. 1 foot 4 inches − 9 inches = _____

Directions Multiply these measurements.

11. 4 yards 1 foot 3 inches
   ×   4

12. 10 feet 5 inches
   ×   3

13. 2 × (3 feet 2 inches) = _____

14. 3 × (3 yards 2 feet 7 inches) = _____

15. 8 × (7 yards 3 feet) = _____

Directions Divide these measurements.

16. (18 yards 24 feet 9 inches) ÷ 3 = _____

17. (4 yards 2 feet 8 inches) ÷ 2 = _____

18. (66 yards 33 feet 11 inches) ÷ 11 = _____

19. (24 yards 8 feet 16 inches) ÷ 8 = _____

20. (25 yards 15 feet 5 inches) ÷ 5 = _____

Perimeter

EXAMPLE   Add the lengths of all sides to get perimeter.

2 + 2 + 2 = 6 in.

2 in. ◁△▷ 2 in.
2 in.

Directions Find the perimeter of each shape.

1.
7 in.
4 in.   4 in.
7 in.

5.
10 in.
6 in.
2 in.   2 in.
6 in.
3 in.   3 in.
6 in.

9.
5 in.
10 in.   6 in.
5 in.   10 in.
6 in.

_____

2.
5 in.
4 in.
8 in.
4 in.
4 in.
9 in.

6.
2.5 in.   3 in.
3 in.   2.5 in.
3 in.   3 in.
3 in.

10.
7 in.   7 in.
9 in.

_____

3.
3 in.
3 in.   3 in.
3 in.   3 in.
3 in.

7.
3 in.
5 in.   4 in.
4 in.   4 in.
5 in.

_____

4.
2 in.   2 in.
2 in.   2 in.
3 in.

8.
4 in.
4 in.   4 in.
4 in.
4 in.   4 in.
4 in.   4 in.
4 in.   4 in.
4 in.

_____

Area

Multiply length by width to find the area.

$$L \times W = A$$
$$9 \times 3 = A$$
$$27 \text{ square feet} = A$$

3 ft

9 ft

Directions Find the area of each rectangle.

1. 30 in.

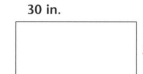

20 in.

_____

5.

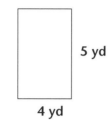

5 yd

4 yd

_____

9.

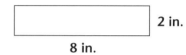

2 in.

8 in.

_____

2.

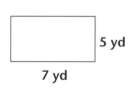

5 yd

7 yd

_____

6.

6 mi

12 mi

_____

10.

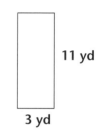

11 yd

3 yd

_____

3.

4 ft

1 ft

_____

7.

2.5 ft

10 ft

_____

4.

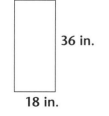

36 in.

18 in.

_____

8.

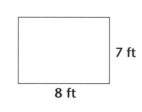

7 ft

8 ft

_____

Area of Triangles

EXAMPLE   Find the area of a triangle whose base is 24 feet and height is 7 feet.

Area $= \frac{1}{2}$ base $\times$ height

$A = \frac{1}{2}(24) \times 7$

$A = 12 \times 7$

$A = 84$ square feet

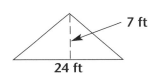

7 ft

24 ft

Directions Find the area of each triangle described below.

1. base = 16 feet

     height = 6 feet   _____

2. base = 41 feet

     height = 32 feet   _____

3. base = 40 feet

     height = 10 feet   _____

4. base = 50 feet

     height = 12 feet   _____

5. base = 12 feet

     height = 10 feet   _____

6. base = 5 feet

     height = 4 feet   _____

7. base = 20 inches

     height = 10 inches   _____

8. base = 33 inches

     height = 50 inches   _____

9. base = 9 yards

     height = 18 yards   _____

10. base = 10 yards

     height = 15 yards   _____

11. base = 6 inches

     height = 17 inches   _____

12. base = 3 yards

     height = 20 yards   _____

13. base = $\frac{2}{3}$ inch

     height = 12 inches   _____

14. base = $\frac{3}{4}$ foot

     height = 16 feet   _____

15. base = $1\frac{1}{8}$ inches

     height = 6 inches   _____

16. base = 10 yards

     height = $4\frac{1}{2}$ yards   _____

17. base = 20 yards

     height = 5 yards   _____

18. base = 10 feet

     height = 2 feet   _____

19. base = $\frac{1}{2}$ inch

     height = $\frac{1}{16}$ inch   _____

20. base = $1\frac{1}{16}$ inches

     height = 6 inches   _____

Area of Parallelograms

To find area of a parallelogram, multiply base by height.

Area = base × height

$A = bh$ $b = 5$ in. $h = 7$ in.

$A = 5 \times 7$

$A = 35$ square inches

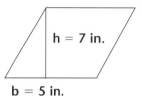

Directions Find the area of each parallelogram.

1.
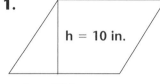

Area = _____

2.
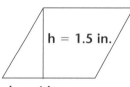

Area = _____

3.
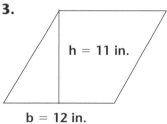

Area = _____

4.
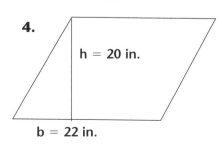

Area = _____

5.
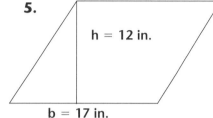

Area = _____

6. base = 20 feet
height = 30 feet

Area = _____

7. base = 34 yards
height = 10 yards

Area = _____

8. base = 4 inches
height = 14 inches

Area = _____

9. base = 12 feet
height = 6 feet

Area = _____

10. base = 21 miles
height = 2 miles

Area = _____

11. base = 1 foot
height = 1 foot

Area = _____

12. base = 14 inches
height = 1 foot

Area = _____

13. base = 4.5 inches
height = 4 inches

Area = _____

14. base = 5 inches
height = 1 foot

Area = _____

15. base = 3 yards
height = 4 feet

Area = _____

Volume of Rectangular Prisms

EXAMPLE   Multiply length by width by height to find volume.

Volume = area of base × height

        = length × width × height

        = 5 in. × 6 in. × 7 in.

        = 30 square inches × 7 in.

        = 210 cubic inches

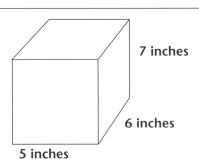

7 inches

6 inches

5 inches

Directions Compute the volume for these prisms. Express your answers in cubic units.

1.

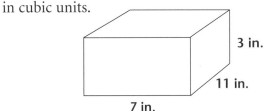

3 in.

11 in.

7 in.

Volume = _____

2.

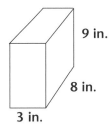

9 in.

8 in.

3 in.

Volume = _____

3.

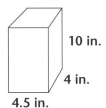

10 in.

4 in.

4.5 in.

Volume = _____

4.

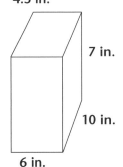

7 in.

10 in.

6 in.

Volume = _____

5. length = 20 yards
width = 7 yards
height = 4 yards

Volume = _____

6. length = 2 feet
width = 5 feet
height = 10 feet

Volume = _____

7. length = 15 feet
width = 7 feet
height = 5 feet

Volume = _____

8. length = 13 feet
width = 5 feet
height = 2 feet

Volume = _____

9. length = 6 in.
width = 14 in.
height = 4 in.

Volume = _____

10. length = 10 in.
width = 12 in.
height = 9 in.

Volume = _____

Volume of Triangular Prisms

EXAMPLE

Multiply $\frac{1}{2}$ area of base by height to find volume.

Volume $= \frac{1}{2}$ (base $\times$ height) Height

$= \frac{1}{2}$ (10 $\times$ 12) $\times$ 14

$= \frac{1}{2}$ (120) $\times$ 14

$= 60 \times 14$

$= 840$ cubic inches

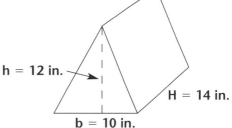

h = 12 in.

H = 14 in.

b = 10 in.

Directions Find the volume of these triangular prisms.

1.

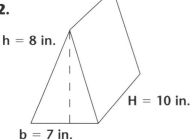

h = 8 in.

H = 10 in.

b = 6 in.

Volume = _____

4.

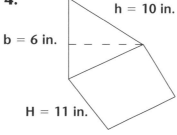

h = 10 in.

b = 6 in.

H = 11 in.

Volume = _____

7. base = 30 inches
height = 10 inches
Height = 15 inches

Volume = _____

8. base = 40 inches
height = 10 inches
Height = 20 inches

Volume = _____

2.

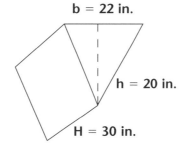

h = 8 in.

H = 10 in.

b = 7 in.

Volume = _____

5.

b = 22 in.

h = 20 in.

H = 30 in.

Volume = _____

9. base = 16 inches
height = 12 inches
Height = 22 inches

Volume = _____

10. base = 20 inches
height = 15 inches
Height = 17 inches

Volume = _____

3.

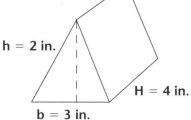

h = 2 in.

H = 4 in.

b = 3 in.

Volume = _____

6.

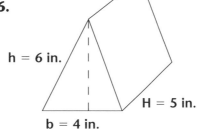

h = 6 in.

H = 5 in.

b = 4 in.

Volume = _____

Finding Circumference

EXAMPLE Find the circumference of a circle with a radius of 5 inches.

Circumference = π × d where π = 3.14

C = 3.14 × 10 because diameter = 2 × radius

C = 31.4 inches

Remember to multiply the radius by 2 to get the diameter for the formula. C = π × d

---

Directions Find the circumference of these circles.

1.

r = 3

C = _____

3.

d = 8

C = _____

5.

r = 13

C = _____

2.

d = 12

C = _____

4.

r = 17

C = _____

6.

d = 9

C = _____

7. diameter = 22

Circumference = _____

9. radius = 16

Circumference = _____

8. diameter = 25

Circumference = _____

10. radius = 20

Circumference = _____

Area and Circumference of Circles

EXAMPLES   Find the area and circumference of a circle with a radius of 5 inches.

Area $= \pi r^2$ Circumference $= 2 \pi r$
$\quad = 3.14 \times 5^2$ $\quad = 2 \times 3.14 \times 5$
$\quad = 3.14 \times 25$ $\quad = 31.4$ inches
$\quad = 78.50$ square inches

Directions Solve for the area and circumference for each circle.
Use 3.14 for π. The abbreviation for circumference is C.

1.

Area = _____

C = _____

5.

Area = _____

C = _____

9.

Area = _____

C = _____

13.

Area = _____

C = _____

2.

Area = _____

C = _____

6.

Area = _____

C = _____

10.

Area = _____

C = _____

14.

Area = _____

C = _____

3.

Area = _____

C = _____

7.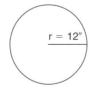

Area = _____

C = _____

11.

Area = _____

C = _____

15.

Area = _____

C = _____

4.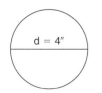

Area = _____

C = _____

8.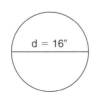

Area = _____

C = _____

12.

Area = _____

C = _____

Volume of a Cylinder

EXAMPLE   Volume = π r² H

r = 3

H = 10

Volume = π × 3² × 10

= 3.14 × 9 × 10

= 3.14 × 90

= 282.6 cubic units

Remember volume is expressed as cubic units.

Directions Find the volume for each cylinder.

1.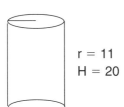

r = 11
H = 20

V = _____

3.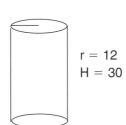

r = 12
H = 30

V = _____

5.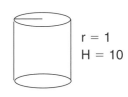

r = 1
H = 10

V = _____

2.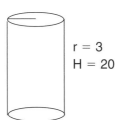

r = 3
H = 20

V = _____

4.

r = 9
H = 2

V = _____

6.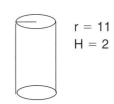

r = 11
H = 2

V = _____

7. radius = 11

height = 10

Volume = _____

9. radius = 20

height = 22

Volume = _____

8. radius = 10

height = 15

Volume = _____

10. radius = 8

height = 18

Volume = _____

Units of Time

$\boxed{\text{EXAMPLE}}$ Add.   5 weeks   3 days
                       +   4 days
                        _____
                       5 weeks   7 days = 6 weeks

Directions   Perform the indicated operations. Simplify the answers.

1.   6 weeks   4 days
     +   4 days
     _____

2.   3 years   2 weeks   6 days
     + 2 years   6 weeks   3 days
     _____

3.   7 weeks   4 days
     + 2 weeks   5 days
     _____

4.   9 weeks   5 days
     − 7 weeks   6 days
     _____

5.   8 years   6 weeks   3 days
     − 3 years   5 weeks   6 days
     _____

6.   5 weeks   3 days
     −   6 days
     _____

7.   15 years   9 weeks
     −   7 years   7 weeks
     _____

8.   10 years   2 weeks   1 day
     −   8 years   5 weeks   4 days
     _____

9.   3 days   12 hours   10 min
     + 3 days   7 hours   56 min
     _____

10.   5 hours   10 min   5 sec
      + 8 hours   50 min   58 sec
      _____

11.   2 hours   20 min   4 sec
      −   1 hour   10 min   7 sec
      _____

12.   4 hours   10 min   5 sec
      − 3 hours   9 min   5 sec
      _____

13.   3 hours   2 min
      − 2 hours   8 min
      _____

14.   7 hours   8 sec
      − 6 hours   10 min
      _____

15. 3 days = _____ hours

16. 18 minutes = _____ seconds

17. 3 years = _____ weeks

18. 180 seconds = _____ minutes

19. 5 weeks 3 days − 3 weeks 5 days 3 hours = _____

20. 8 years 8 weeks 2 days + 2 years 9 weeks 5 days = _____

21. 4 hours 3 min 34 sec − 2 hours 7 min 50 sec = _____

22. 5 min 45 sec + 5 hours 4 min 49 sec = _____

23. 35 hours 24 sec − 9 hours 28 min = _____

24. 55 min 19 sec + 1 hour 20 min 4 sec = _____

25. 36 hours − 3 hours 5 min 6 sec = _____

Time Problems

You can solve word problems involving elapsed time by adding
or subtracting time. You may need to rename in some problems.
Remember that there are 60 minutes in one hour.

EXAMPLE Mr. Winkle went to sleep at 11:25 last night. He looked at the
clock when he woke up. How long did he sleep?

$$
\begin{array}{rcl}
7{:}43 & = & 19{:}43 \\
-\,11{:}25 & = & -\,11{:}25 \\
\hline
 & & 8{:}18
\end{array}
$$
  Mr. Winkle slept 8 hours and 18 minutes.

Directions Solve each word problem. Use the clock shown with each
problem to help you.

1. Tanya started to play
tennis at 9:30. How long
has she been playing?

2. Emily left for the ocean
at 7:45. She saw a clock
when she arrived. How
long was the trip?

3. A video lasts 117
minutes. At what time
will it be finished?

4. The roast is to cook for
2 hours and 15 minutes.
At what time will it be
finished cooking?

5. We can play for another
half of an hour. At what
time must we come in?

6. Carmine's favorite program
comes on at 8:30. How long
until it starts?

7. Niki arrived at the doctor's
office at 8:45. She glanced
at the clock when her name
was called. How long did
she wait?

8. Jared started the meeting
at 10:15. Afterward, he
looked at the clock. How
long was the meeting?

9. The bus from Duluth will
arrive at 3:23. How long
until it arrives?

10. Carlos put money in
the parking meter for $1\frac{1}{2}$
hours. When must he
return?

Reading Pictographs

EXAMPLE

Look at the pictograph below.

One book is equal to 4 books read.
How many books did Andy read?
3 whole books are pictured.
$3 \times 4 = 12$

Andy read 12 books.

Summer Book Reading Club

[ ] = 4 books read

Andy

Megan

Sue

Vinnee

Filson

Leona

Directions Use the pictograph to answer the questions.

1. How many books did Megan read for the summer? _____

2. How many books did Sue read? _____

3. How many books did Filson read? Did he read more than Andy? _____

4. How many books did Vinnee read? _____

5. How many books did Sue and Andy read? _____

6. What was the total number of books read by the club? _____

7. What is the title of this graph? _____

8. How many books would Megan need to read to match Filson's total? _____

9. How many books did Leona read? _____

10. How many did both Leona and Megan read? _____

Constructing Bar Graphs

EXAMPLE   January = 5 inches

Find January on the horizontal line.

Find 5 on the vertical line.

Shade the bar from the horizontal line to 5.

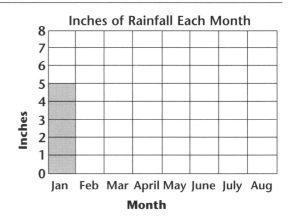

Directions Shade the data for each bar of the graphs.

Jan = 3 inches

Feb = 5 inches

March = 4 inches

April = 2 inches

May = 6 inches

June = 5 inches

July = 8 inches

Aug = 5 inches

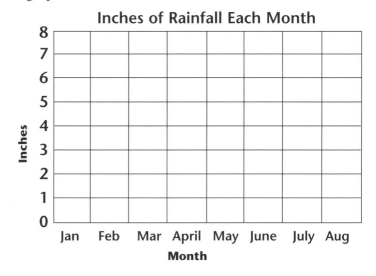

Jan = 6 inches

Feb = 3 inches

March = 7 inches

April = 1 inches

May = 4.5 inches

June = 8 inches

July = 3.5 inches

Aug = 1.5 inches

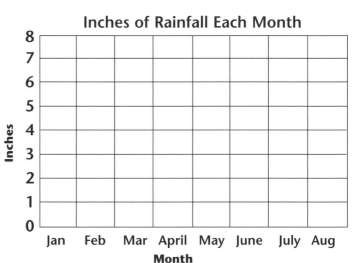

Reading Divided Bar Graphs

EXAMPLE

How many trucks are in Lot F?

Find F on the graph.
Determine the scale.
Read the key.
The scale in each section equals 25 vehicles.
Trucks make up 6 sections.

$25 \times 6 = 150$ 150 trucks are in Lot F.

Directions Use the divided bar graph to answer the questions.

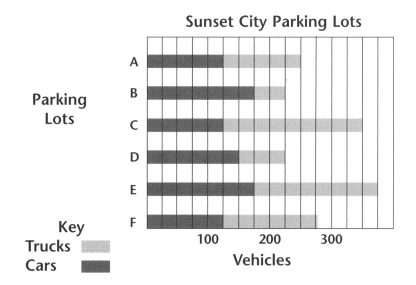

Sunset City Parking Lots

Parking Lots: A, B, C, D, E, F

Key
Trucks
Cars

Vehicles

1. How many trucks are parked in Lot D? _____

2. How many cars are located in Lot B? _____

3. How many vehicles are in Lot F? _____

4. How many trucks are in Lot A? _____

5. How many vehicles are in Lot C? _____

6. How many vehicles are in Lot D? _____

7. How many cars are parked in Lot E? _____

8. How many vehicles are shown for Lots D and E together? _____

9. How many vehicles are shown for Lots A and B together? _____

10. How many vehicles are parked in Sunset City parking lots? _____

Constructing Divided Bar Graphs

EXAMPLE

How many points did Mattie score on the first test?

Find Mattie on the graph.
Determine the scale.
Read the key.
The scale is 1 section equals 1 point.
Mattie's first test shows 9 sections.
Mattie scored 9 points.

Directions Use the divided bar graph to answer the questions.

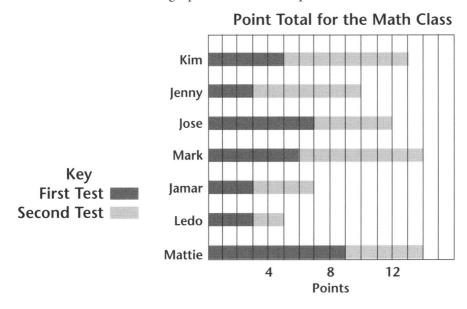

Point Total for the Math Class

Key
First Test
Second Test

1. Did Jamar score more total points than Jenny? _____

2. How many total points did Jose score? _____

3. How many points did Ledo score on the first test? _____

4. How many points did Kim score on the second test? _____

5. What are the total points accumulated for Mark and Kim? _____

6. What are the total points accumulated for all the students? _____

7. What are the total points for Jenny and Mark on the second test? _____

8. What are the total points scored on the first test? _____

9. What is the difference between the first and second test totals? _____

10. What was Ledo's total point accumulation? _____

Reading Line Graphs

 EXAMPLE

How many tickets were sold in January?

Find January (Jan) on the graph.
Use a straightedge to align the point for January with the vertical line.
Read the number.
150 tickets were sold in January.

Directions Use the line graph to answer the questions about the school's
raffle ticket sale.

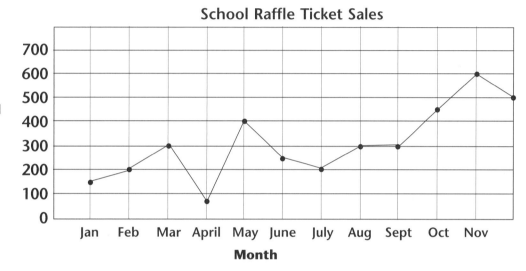

School Raffle Ticket Sales

1. Were there more tickets sold in May than October? _____

2. How many tickets were sold in May? October? _____

3. How many tickets were sold in March? _____

4. How many tickets were sold in the summer months
   of June and July? _____

5. What month had the highest sales? _____

6. What month had the lowest sales? _____

7. How many more tickets were sold in May than July? _____

8. How many tickets were sold in February? _____

9. How many tickets were sold in June? _____

10. What was the total number of tickets sold? _____

Circle Graphs

EXAMPLE   The Davises have an annual income of $24,000.00.
How much do they spend on food?

Find the section labeled food and identify its percent of the budget.

Multiply. $24,000.00 × 30% =
$24,000.00 × 0.30 = $7,200.00

Directions   Answer the following questions about this graph.
Use an annual income of $24,000 for problems 2–4.

1. What do the members of the Davis family spend most of their money on? _____

2. How much do they spend for clothing? _____

3. How much do they save each year? _____

4. What do they spend for entertainment? _____

5. How much do the Davises spend for each category
in their budget if their annual income is $48,400.00?

Food _____   Clothing _____   Transportation _____

Housing _____   Savings _____   Entertainment _____

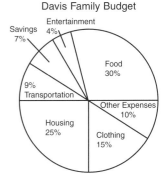

Davis Family Budget

Directions   Make a circle graph to show the information in the table below.
Follow these six steps:

Step 1   Draw a large circle. Mark the center of the circle
with a dot.

Step 2   Draw a radius.

Step 3   Find out how many degrees are in each sector.
To find the degrees, multiply the percent or fraction
by the 360° in a circle. (Example: 360° × 10% = 36°)

Step 4   Use a protractor to measure and draw each sector.
Use the center of the circle
as the vertex of each angle.

Step 5   Label each sector and
mark the appropriate
percent or fraction.

Step 6   Give the graph a title.

The Thomas Family Budget	
Category	**Percent Allowed**
Food	25%
Housing	30%
Clothing	20%
Car	10%
Savings	5%
Other	10%

Graphs That Mislead

EXAMPLE

Draw a bar showing 3 games won in September on each graph.

Find September on the graphs. Give a title for the graphs. Shade sections to show 3 games in each graph.

Directions Make the bar graphs below. Then answer the questions on your own paper.

Walbrook High School basketball stats for the current school year	
Month	**Games won**
September	2 games
October	3 games
November	4 games
December	5 games
January	6 games
February	8 games
March	7 games

1. Construct 2 bar graphs for the data. Use the templates given below.

2. Give a title for each graph.

3. How do the graphs differ?

4. Why does graph 2 look better than graph 1?

5. Does one graph represent the data better than the other? Explain.

Scale Models

EXAMPLE   The building block shown below is a scale model of a much bigger block
using 1:50 scale. How long is the actual block?

$$\frac{1}{50} = \frac{12}{n}$$

$50 \times 12 = n$

$600 \text{ mm} = n$ 600 mm is the length of the actual building block.

Directions Use the model to solve each problem.

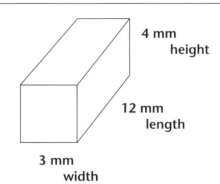

4 mm
height

12 mm
length

3 mm
width

1. The ratio is changed to 1:25.

   a. Solve for the actual length.   _____

   b. Solve for the actual width.   _____

   c. Solve for the actual height.   _____

2. Solve for all three components if the ratio is 1:75.

_____   _____   _____

3. Solve for all three components if the ratio is 1:200.

_____   _____   _____

4. Solve for all three components if the ratio is 1:100.

_____   _____   _____

5. Solve for all three components if the ratio is 1:80.

_____   _____   _____

Scale Drawings

EXAMPLE   The wagon below measures $\frac{1}{2}$ inch high and $2\frac{1}{2}$ inches long.

The scale ratio is 1:50. How long is the actual wagon?

$$\frac{1}{50} = \frac{2\frac{1}{2}}{n}$$

$$2\frac{1}{2} \times 50 = n$$

$$\frac{5}{2} \times 50 = \frac{250}{2} = 125$$

125 inches = n The actual wagon is 125 inches long.

Directions Use the model to solve each problem.

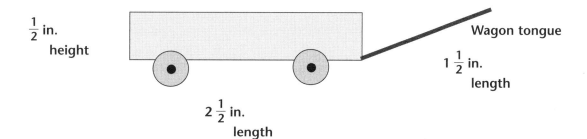

$\frac{1}{2}$ in.
height

Wagon tongue

$1\frac{1}{2}$ in.
length

$2\frac{1}{2}$ in.
length

1. Solve for the actual height of the wagon if the scale is 1:50.   _____

2. Solve for the actual height of the wagon if the scale is 1:25.   _____

3. Solve for the actual length of the wagon with a scale of 1:100.   _____

4. How long is the wagon tongue if the scale is 1:50?   _____

5. How long is the wagon tongue if the scale is 1:25?   _____

Floor Plans

EXAMPLE The scale is 1 inch for each 8 feet. Find the actual dimensions of this drawing in feet.

Find the length.

Set up a proportion.

$\dfrac{1}{8} = \dfrac{6}{n}$

$8 \times 6 = n$

48 feet $= n$ Actual length is 48 feet.

Find the width.

Set up a proportion.

$\dfrac{1}{8} = \dfrac{3}{n}$

$8 \times 3 = n$

24 feet $= n$ Actual width is 24 feet.

Scale

1 inch = 8 feet

width = 3 inches

length = 6 inches

Directions Use proportions to solve each problem.

1. Find the actual measurements in feet of a room drawing that measures 4 inches by 5 inches with a scale of 1 inch = 3 feet.

length _____   width _____

2. Find the actual measurements in feet of a room drawing that measures 3 inches by 4 inches with a scale of 1 inch = 4 feet.

length _____   width _____

3. Scale of 1 inch = 5 feet

length = 4 inches

width = 3 inches

actual length = _____

actual width = _____

4. Scale of 1 inch = 4 feet

length = 7 inches

width = 6 inches

actual length = _____

actual width = _____

5. Scale of 1 inch = 6 feet

length = 5 inches

width = 3 inches

actual length = _____

actual width = _____

Map Distances

EXAMPLE   Use a scale of 1 inch = 500 miles.

Solve for the actual distance between two cities if they measure $3\frac{1}{2}$ inches apart.

$3\frac{1}{2} \times 500$ = actual distance

$\frac{7}{2} \times 500$ = actual distance

$\frac{3,500}{2}$ = actual distance

1,750 miles   The actual distance is 1,750 miles.

Directions Use the information to solve each problem.

1. scale of 1 inch = 600 miles

measured distance of $2\frac{1}{2}$ inches

actual distance = _____

2. scale of 1 inch = 500 miles

measured distance of $3\frac{1}{2}$ inches

actual distance = _____

3. scale of 1 inch = 400 miles

measured distance of 5 inches

actual distance = _____

4. scale of 1 inch = 14 miles

measured distance of 6 inches

actual distance = _____

5. scale of 1 inch = 13 miles

measured distance of $4\frac{1}{2}$ inches

actual distance = _____

6. scale of 1 inch = 35 miles

measured distance of $4\frac{1}{2}$ inches

actual distance = _____

7. scale of 1 inch = 40 miles

measured distance of 7 inches

actual distance = _____

8. scale of 1 inch = $12\frac{1}{2}$ miles

measured distance of 6 inches

actual distance = _____

9. scale of 1 inch = 100 miles

measured distance of 3 inches

actual distance = _____

10. scale of 1 inch = 200 miles

measured distance of $1\frac{1}{2}$ inches

actual distance = _____

Integers

Compare the numbers using < and >.

| 1 | 5 | < means less than. Read 1 is less than 5. | 1 < 5 |
| 6 | 2 | > means more than. Read 6 is more than 2. | 6 > 2 |

Directions Use the number line to help you compare the integers in each pair using < or >.

1. −1	8	**6.** −9	−5	**11.** −11	−1	**16.** −5	0
2. −1	−2	**7.** +1	−3	**12.** −1	0	**17.** −3	−5
3. 3	−3	**8.** 0	−9	**13.** 0	−19	**18.** +7	−1
4. +4	−5	**9.** −4	+2	**14.** −1	+1	**19.** −34	+32
5. +5	+9	**10.** −4	−5	**15.** −8	+1	**20.** +19	−1

Directions Find the sum of these integers.

21. $0 + 3$ _____   **24.** $-3 + 3$ _____   **27.** $-9 + 0$ _____

22. $-8 + 8$ _____   **25.** $-1 + 1$ _____   **28.** $-1 + 0$ _____

23. $+9 + (-9)$ _____   **26.** $-2 + 2$ _____

Directions Name the opposite of each integer.

29. −23 _____   **32.** 0 _____   **35.** −29 _____   **38.** −201 _____

30. +54 _____   **33.** +33 _____   **36.** −211 _____   **39.** −101 _____

31. −1 _____   **34.** +1 _____   **37.** +22 _____   **40.** +46 _____

Adding Positive and Negative Integers

EXAMPLE Find the sum of 2 and (−8).

Begin at 2 on the number line. Move 8 places left.

$$-7 \quad -6 \quad -5 \quad -4 \quad -3 \quad -2 \quad -1 \quad 0 \quad +1 \quad +2 \quad +3 \quad +4 \quad +5 \quad +6 \quad +7$$

$2 + (−8) = −6$

Directions Use a number line to help find each sum.

1. $+3 + (−7)$ _____

2. $−3 + (+2)$ _____

3. $−3 + (+8)$ _____

4. $−9 + (−1)$ _____

5. $−3 + (−1)$ _____

6. $−7 + (+1)$ _____

7. $−1 + (−1)$ _____

8. $−9 + (+1)$ _____

9. $−3 + (+9)$ _____

10. $+2 + (+4)$ _____

11. $+8 + (−1)$ _____

12. $+2 + (−2)$ _____

13. $−11 + (−12)$ _____

14. $−10 + (−10)$ _____

15. $−1 + 0$ _____

16. $−13 + (−12)$ _____

17. $+11 + (−21)$ _____

18. $−19 + (+10)$ _____

19. $+12 + (−16)$ _____

20. $−14 + (+1)$ _____

Directions Give the absolute value for each number.

21. $|−3|$ _____

22. $|+12|$ _____

23. $|−1|$ _____

24. $|−11|$ _____

25. $|−6|$ _____

26. $|−77|$ _____

27. $|+8|$ _____

28. $|−99|$ _____

29. $|+22|$ _____

30. $|−202|$ _____

31. $|−33|$ _____

32. $|+17|$ _____

33. $|+21|$ _____

34. $|−28|$ _____

35. $|+102|$ _____

36. $|+38|$ _____

37. $|+51|$ _____

38. $|−18|$ _____

39. $|−111|$ _____

40. $|−90|$ _____

Subtracting Positive and Negative Integers

EXAMPLES   Change subtraction problems to addition of the opposite.

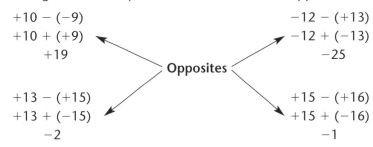

$+10 - (-9)$
$+10 + (+9)$
$+19$

$-12 - (+13)$
$-12 + (-13)$
-25

Opposites

$+13 - (+15)$
$+13 + (-15)$
-2

$+15 - (+16)$
$+15 + (-16)$
-1

Directions Solve these subtraction problems by changing to adding the opposite.

1. $+1 - (-12)$ _____

2. $+22 - (-12)$ _____

3. $+10 - (-12)$ _____

4. $+20 - (-12)$ _____

5. $-9 - (+11)$ _____

6. $-31 - (+20)$ _____

7. $+21 - (-20)$ _____

8. $+3 - (+3)$ _____

9. $-29 - (+23)$ _____

10. $-21 - (+21)$ _____

11. $+34 - (-23)$ _____

12. $+56 - (-40)$ _____

13. $-31 - (-13)$ _____

14. $-90 - (+41)$ _____

15. $+26 - (-50)$ _____

16. $-11 - (-51)$ _____

17. $-14 - (-33)$ _____

18. $-10 - (-22)$ _____

19. $-28 - (+1)$ _____

20. $-10 - (-40)$ _____

21. $+20 - (-50)$ _____

22. $-18 - (+7)$ _____

23. $-21 - (-22)$ _____

24. $-20 - (+20)$ _____

25. $+2 - (-1) - (-2) - (+11)$ _____

26. $+1 - (-3) - (+3) - (-10)$ _____

27. $-10 - (-11) - (+12) - (-12)$ _____

28. $-1 - (+1) - (+2) - (-3)$ _____

29. $+12 - (-10) - (-11) - (+20)$ _____

30. $+11 - (-10) - (-1) - (+2)$ _____

Word Problems

EXAMPLE Subtract by adding the opposite.
$-19 - (+10) + (-15)$
$-19 + (-10) + (-15) = -44$

Directions Find these sums and differences.

1. $-2 - (+4) + (-7) - (+8)$ _____

2. $-1 + (+33) + (-10) - (-10)$ _____

3. $-10 + (-12) + (+19) - (-2)$ _____

4. $+3 - (+4) - (+5) - (-7)$ _____

5. $-4 - (-7) + (+10) + (-8)$ _____

6. $+15 - (+16) + (+10)$ _____

7. $+11 - (-11) + (+10)$ _____

8. $-19 - (-19) + (+8)$ _____

9. $+2 - (-1) - (+7) - (+8)$ _____

10. $+11 + (-10) - (+13)$ _____

Directions Write an addition sentence for each problem in the space provided and solve.

11. Marline's saving account had $750.00 and she withdrew $20.00 on Monday. She deposited $100.00 on Tuesday. Wednesday she wrote a check for $12.90. Thursday she deposited her paycheck of $175.50. Friday she deposited $100.00. How much was her final balance on Friday?

_____

12. Starting at 70 degrees, if the temperature goes up 20 degrees, then drops 10 degrees, then goes up 14 degrees, what is the new temperature?

_____

13. Milo spent $30.00 for food and $13.75 for camping supplies. He was paid $12.00 for the trip. How much does he have?

_____

14. Dante had the following expenses for his Lawn Care Service: $2.75, $5.00, $10.00, $8.00. He was paid $22.00, $25.00, $15.00, and $18.00. How much did he make after expenses?

_____

15. Teresa spent $5.95 at one store, $6.32 at another, and $15.98 at a third store. If she had $35.00 before shopping, how much does she have left?

_____

Multiplying Positive and Negative Integers

EXAMPLES   The product of two numbers with like signs will be positive.

$-3(-4) = +12$ $+2(+4) = +8$

The product of two numbers with unlike signs will be negative.

$-3(+7) = -21$ $+4(-10) = -40$

Directions Write the factor to make a correct sentence.

1. $-4(\quad) = -16$

2. $+5(\quad) = +20$

3. $(\quad)(-6) = -18$

4. $-7(\quad) = -14$

5. $-6(\quad) = +24$

6. $(\quad)(+8) = -64$

7. $+19(\quad) = -38$

8. $(\quad)(-22) = +66$

9. $-1(\quad) = -1$

10. $+12(\quad) = -36$

11. $+9(\quad) = -27$

12. $(\quad)(+4) = -48$

13. $-2(\quad)(-5) = -30$

14. $(\quad)(-3)(+5) = +45$

15. $+5(+2)(\quad) = -20$

Directions Solve for the product.

16. $-5(-6) =$ _____

17. $-4(+5) =$ _____

18. $+7(-5) =$ _____

19. $-23(+2) =$ _____

20. $-2(-3)(-4) =$ _____

21. $+3(-6)(-1) =$ _____

22. $-9(+2)(-2) =$ _____

23. $-7(-7)(+2) =$ _____

24. $+9(-3)(-1) =$ _____

25. $+5(-5)(-5) =$ _____

26. $-1(-1)(-1)(-1) =$ _____

27. $+2(-8)(-2)(-1) =$ _____

28. $-4(+8)(-2) =$ _____

29. $-3(+3)(-1)(-1) =$ _____

30. $-7(+3)(+2) =$ _____

Properties of Addition and Multiplication

EXAMPLES

Commutative Property of Addition and Multiplication
$$7 + 8 = 8 + 7$$
$$15 = 15 \quad \text{Both sums equal 15.}$$

$$-3 \times (-4) = -4 \times (-3)$$
$$+12 = +12 \quad \text{Both products equal } +12.$$

Associative Property of Addition and Multiplication
$$(6 + 2) + 8 = 6 + (2 + 8)$$
$$8 + 8 = 6 + 10$$
$$16 = 16$$

$$(5 \times 6) \times 2 = 5 \times (6 \times 2)$$
$$30 \times 2 = 5 \times 12$$
$$60 = 60$$

Distributive Property of Multiplication with Respect to Addition and Subtraction
$$3 \times (2 + 5) = 3 \times 2 + 3 \times 5$$
$$3 \times 7 = 6 + 15$$
$$21 = 21$$

$$4 \times (10 - 3) = 4 \times 10 - 4 \times 3$$
$$4 \times 7 = 40 - 12$$
$$28 = 28$$

Directions Write the property used for each expression.

1. $-2(-4) = -4(-2)$ _____

2. $(2 \times 4) \times 5 = 2 \times (4 \times 5)$ _____

3. $2 \times (15 - 3) = 2 \times 15 - 2 \times 3$ _____

4. $7 + (5 + 4) = (7 + 5) + 4$ _____

5. $11 + 16 = 16 + 11$ _____

6. $+8(+3) = +3(+8)$ _____

7. $(3 + 7) + 8 = 3 + (7 + 8)$ _____

Directions Solve these expressions.

8. $-9 \times (+8) =$

9. $-6(-8) =$

10. $4 \times (12 - 7) =$

11. $23 + (45 + 20) =$

12. $(7 + 19) + 12 =$

13. $(12 + 4) + 3 =$

14. $-15(-10) =$

15. $-3(-8) =$

Dividing Positive and Negative Integers

EXAMPLES   The quotient of two numbers with like signs will be positive.
$-12 \div (-4) = +3$ and $+20 \div (+5) = +4$
Both answers are positive.

The quotient of two numbers with unlike signs will be negative.
$+24 \div (-2) = -12$ $\dfrac{-16}{+2} = -8$

Directions   Solve for the quotients.

1. $-12 \div (+2) = $ _____

2. $-16 \div (+2) = $ _____

3. $+24 \div (+3) = $ _____

4. $-25 \div (-5) = $ _____

5. $+45 \div (-5) = $ _____

6. $+22 \div (-1) = $ _____

7. $+34 \div (-17) = $ _____

8. $+23 \div (+1) = $ _____

9. $-54 \div (-9) = $ _____

10. $+18 \div (-2) = $ _____

11. $-48 \div (+6) = $ _____

12. $-35 \div (-5) = $ _____

13. $+90 \div (-2) = $ _____

14. $+21 \div (-7) = $ _____

15. $+49 \div (-7) = $ _____

16. $-26 \div (-13) = $ _____

17. $-36 \div (+9) = $ _____

18. $-28 \div (+2) = $ _____

19. $\dfrac{-12}{-2} = $ _____

20. $\dfrac{+35}{-7} = $ _____

21. $\dfrac{+60}{-5} = $ _____

22. $\dfrac{-8}{-8} = $ _____

23. $\dfrac{+28}{-4} = $ _____

24. $\dfrac{-40}{+4} = $ _____

25. $\dfrac{+88}{-11} = $ _____

26. $\dfrac{+50}{+5} = $ _____

27. $\dfrac{+44}{-4} = $ _____

28. $\dfrac{-80}{+4} = $ _____

29. $\dfrac{+110}{-11} = $ _____

30. $\dfrac{+24}{+8} = $ _____

Variables and the Number Line

EXAMPLE   Find the number on the number line. Draw a dot there.

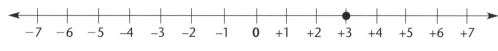

$x = 3$

Directions Graph these values of x on the number lines.

1. $x = 7$

2. $x = -4$

3. $x = -2$

4. $x = +5$

5. $x = -6$

6. $x = -1$

7. $x = -7$

8. $x = -8$

9. $x = 0$

10. $x = 6$

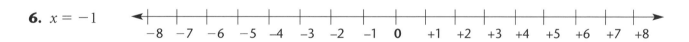

Graphing Coordinates

EXAMPLE   Number the x and y axes and graph the ordered pairs.

Plot (−2, 1).

Find −2 on x on the graph.

Find 1 on y on the graph.

Plot the point where they meet.

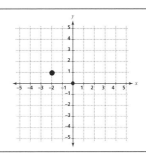

Directions Number the x and y axes and graph the ordered pairs.

1. $(-3, 4)$ $(-5, -5)$ $(1, 4)$ $(0, -3)$ $(4, 0)$

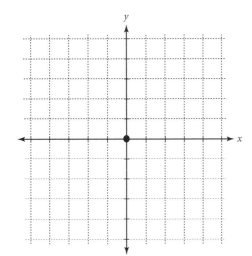

3. $(2, -5)$ $(-1, -1)$ $(-2, 4)$ $(5, -3)$ $(-4, -2)$

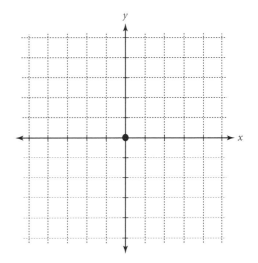

2. $(2, 1)$ $(3, -1)$ $(-2, 5)$ $(-4, 4)$ $(-3, -4)$

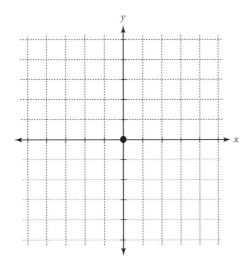

4. $(0, -1)$ $(0, 4)$ $(-4, 0)$ $(-1, 3)$ $(-4, 1)$

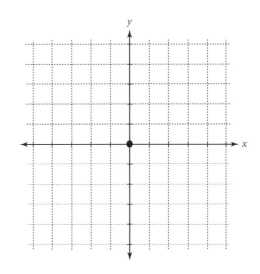

Solving Equations by Adding and Subtracting

EXAMPLE Solve the equation. $x - 19 = +2$

$x - 19 = \;\;+2$

$\underline{+19 = +19}$

$x + 0 = +21$

$\qquad x = +21$

Directions Solve for the variable. Show steps.

1. $x - 2 = 10$

2. $x + 2 = 12$

3. $x - 10 = 12$

4. $x - 10 = -19$

5. $x + 8 = -2$

6. $x - 10 = 20$

7. $x + 2 = -11$

8. $-3 + x = -9$

9. $4 + x = -13$

10. $y - 12 = -3$

11. $-9 + y = -23$

12. $11 = x - 10$

13. $y + 1 = -12$

14. $8 = x - 11$

15. $h - 13 = -23$

Solving Equations by Multiplying and Dividing

EXAMPLE   Solve the equation. $-2x = 38$

$$-2x = 38$$

$$\frac{-2x}{-2} = \frac{38}{-2}$$

$$x = -19$$

Directions Solve for the variable. Show your work.

1. $4x = 20$

2. $5x = 25$

3. $7x = 56$

4. $9x = 81$

5. $8y = 72$

6. $8f = 96$

7. $12x = 144$

8. $6x = 66$

9. $\frac{x}{5} = 8$

10. $\frac{y}{3} = 9$

11. $\frac{k}{8} = 12$

12. $\frac{y}{10} = 14$

13. $-7x = 42$

14. $\frac{k}{9} = 17$

15. $\frac{x}{-8} = 20$

16. $-7x = 35$

17. $-2x = -46$

18. $\frac{x}{4} = 23$

19. $\frac{y}{-9} = 42$

20. $-3k = 30$

Two-Step Equations

EXAMPLE   Solve for the variable. Subtract 3 from both sides. Then divide each side by 2.

$$2x + 3 = 13$$
$$\underline{\ -3 = -3}$$
$$2x = 10$$
$$\frac{2x}{2} = \frac{10}{2}$$
$$x = 5$$

Directions Solve for the variables. Leave fractional answers as improper fractions. Show your work.

1. $3x + 4 = 14$

_____

_____

$x =$ _____

2. $3y - 2 = 19$

_____

_____

$y =$ _____

3. $3y - 8 = 16$

_____

_____

$y =$ _____

4. $2y - 5 = -37$

_____

_____

$y =$ _____

5. $6x + 1 = 27$

_____

_____

$x =$ _____

6. $8k - 2 = 70$

_____

_____

$k =$ _____

7. $6a - 1 = 22$

_____

_____

$a =$ _____

8. $9a + 1 = 82$

_____

_____

$a =$ _____

9. $7z - 2 = 22$

_____

_____

$z =$ _____

10. $3a - 2 = 42$

_____

_____

$a =$ _____

11. $4a + 1 = 35$

_____

_____

$a =$ _____

12. $-2z - 2 = 33$

_____

_____

$z =$ _____

13. $4x - 5 = 32$

_____

_____

$x =$ _____

14. $7w + 1 = 29$

_____

_____

$w =$ _____

15. $-5k - 7 = 76$

_____

_____

$k =$ _____

Combining Like Terms

EXAMPLE   Combine like terms. Add the two terms. $-2a - 4a$

$-2a$
$\underline{-4a}$
$-6a$ so $-2a - 4a = -6a$

Directions Combine like terms.

1. $-7a - 6a$

2. $+4a - 5a$

3. $-2c - 3c - 4c$

4. $-4v - 3v$

5. $7x + 3x - x$

6. $-x - 4x + 9x$

7. $-2x + 8x - x$

8. $+7x + 2x - 10x$

9. $-10y + 31y - y$

10. $-30f - 11f + 1$

11. $-17y + 20y - 2$

12. $4 - 8a - 3a$

13. $-x - x + 4$

14. $+4c - 7c - c$

15. $23c - 8c + c$

16. $9 - 17c + 5c$

17. $+a + a + 8$

18. $-18y + 17y + 1$

19. $-2a - 3a + 5a$

20. $12 + 12a - 24$

21. $-22 + 20y - y$

22. $+7 + 12a - 7a$

23. $3 - x - x - 2x$

24. $13x - 18x + 1$

25. $1 - 3f + 2f + 3$